REVIVING THE
LEFT

returning society to these fixed ideas. These are values that many ordinary people deploy (or would like to deploy) in their lives, and conservatism exploits this ideal of a person.

Of course, not everyone who is attracted to conservative rhetoric about values self-identifies as a conservative. Most people do not organize their moral identities around political ideologies. Yet, conservatism has effectively captured many independent voters because conservative rhetoric reinforces basic themes in the everyday morality and cultural context of ordinary Americans. It articulates a moral framework that clearly links personal virtue with a conception of the public good—a straightforward account of how one's private life contributes to the quality of culture and how the quality of culture contributes to one's private life.

I argue in part 1 that the conservative battle against evil is deeply misguided, as is the assumption that self-reliance and traditional values are capable of effectively confronting evil. The accumulation of political power by this ideology has produced a culture in which social trust and common decency are in short supply and moral catastrophe is a persistent threat. The fact that conservatism has become such a disaster, however, should induce pangs of perplexity and self-doubt among liberals. Why have liberals been unable to mount a counterattack based on the moral foundations of liberalism? The short answer is that we lack a richly textured ideal of a liberal person that can compete with the conservative ideal of a person. Liberalism's failures, in this regard, are the consequence of fundamental assumptions about the relationship between politics and morality that run deep in the liberal tradition that must be revised if liberalism is to revive its moral credentials. Part 2 of this book traces the consequences of these assumptions and outlines the moral foundations of a progressive liberalism that will blunt the force of the conservative "values agenda."

The conservative accusation that liberals lack a conception of evil or the character to confront it is nonsense. It is a figment of the feverish imaginations of culture warriors lounging in right-wing think tanks, gorging themselves on foie gras and Dom Perignon while penning encomia to Bud Light and corn dogs. Liberalism's battle against authoritarianism, tyranny, and human degradation is well documented; we do not need moral advice from corrupt apologists for the venality that today passes for conservatism. However, liberal thought has not adequately articulated its own version of a personal morality, its own account of how liberal persons and their way of life produce social benefit. Liberalism, though grounded in deeply held moral convictions about social justice and the public good, has failed to link public good with private life. It has failed to demonstrate how a concern for social justice is the natural by-product of the basic themes in everyday morality that guide the lives of ordinary people and inspire their aspirations. Modern liberalism emphasizes the institutional arrangements that manage our political and economic relationships, but tends to ignore questions about how to live, what sort of person one ought to be, or what sort of culture is most desirable, except for insisting that we be tolerant of others in order to encourage social peace. In summary, the ethical basis of liberalism is too thin to generate a comprehensive moral identity. This is not to suggest that liberals do not lead good lives. Rather, the nature of a good life and the values that a good life requires are not a sufficiently explicit part of the conceptual framework that drives the liberal political agenda.

This lack of a comprehensive moral identity has rendered liberalism impotent just when an alternative to conservatism is most needed. According to a poll conducted shortly after the 2004 election by Greenberg Quinlan Rosner Research, only 27 percent of Americans believe that Democrats know what they stand for as a party while 55 percent of Americans believe Republicans know what they stand for, suggesting that Democrats lack a core set of convictions that make their policy proposals intelligible.[8] Of course, since this poll was taken, the Republican coalition has fractured like a windshield meeting asphalt. But can liberalism pick up the pieces?

The problem with liberal conviction is not a dearth of policy proposals, which the policy wonks in the Democratic Party can produce by the terabyte. The problem is not a lack of commitment, though liberal activists are often focused on single issues—abortion, the environment, or poverty—with little inclination to forge alliances. What is lacking is a conception of what unifies these policies and commitments, not only as a vision for America but also as moral imperatives around which individuals construct a life. We advocate tolerance and peace. But, in a world of terrorism and mass migration, the virtues of tolerance and peace will not be obvious unless we show voters how their personal aspirations require tolerance and peace. We want to

As I noted, liberal reluctance to take strong moral stands regarding the kind of lives it is good for human beings to live is motivated by a concern to protect liberty. However, to assume that we can protect liberty without substantive moral commitments involves a misunderstanding of both liberty and morality. Liberty can exist only within a culture of moral responsibility. But such a culture of responsibility can exist only when it develops organically out of relationships of trust and care, rather than the relationships of power and authority that are so beloved by conservatives. Thus, we must formulate a progressive liberalism that clarifies the intimate connection between a culture of responsibility, social justice, and our individual aspirations to lead good lives that can be realized only within such a culture. In short, liberalism needs a politics of moral purpose if it is to rebuild its moral credentials. The ultimate aim of this book is to clarify the conceptual foundations of such a politics and to show how our institutions can embody the trust, care, and responsibility needed to confront twenty-first-century problems.

Conservatives have declared a culture war—a battle for the soul of America. This is a war that liberals would prefer not to fight, for they risk their virtue, the virtue of tolerance, when battle lines are drawn and weapons are locked and loaded (to use Pat Buchanan's unfortunate phrase). However, in engaging this battle for the soul of America, liberals will not be risking their virtue. A progressive liberalism is more than simple tolerance or inclusiveness; it responds to the call of human flourishing and seeks to make available for everyone the social conditions that enable flourishing. And this call can be understood only in moral terms, because our flourishing depends on fostering a culture of responsibility and care that refuses the lure of exploitation, the addiction of violence, the languor of indifference, and the convenience of authoritarianism. Conservatism incubates these contagions that plague human history; only progressive liberalism stands as a cure.

But if conservatism is to be defeated, we must first come to a clearer understanding of the nature of conservatism, the source of its appeal, and most important, the reasons for its failure to create a decent society. We must do a better job of understanding the obstacles to progressive politics and blunt the force of conservatism's deceptive values agenda that has dominated politics for much of the past thirty years. The economist John Kenneth Galbraith famously said, "The modern conservative is engaged in one of man's oldest exercises in moral philosophy; that is, the search for a superior moral justification for selfishness." Galbraith may indeed be right, and the recent economic collapse helps confirm his judgment. But conservative arguments cannot be dismissed as cynical rationalizations since they persuade many sincere and well-intentioned Americans. We must confront their arguments about culture and moral values rather than trying to change the subject. We can win the future, only if we win the debate about how we arrived at this perilous position. I will argue that it is not only bad economics or poorly conceived foreign policy but also bankrupt moral values that have tarnished America's promise. Thus, I turn first to a critique of conservatism's conception of moral value in part 1, which prepares the way for a discussion in part 2 of how liberalism must revise its conception of moral value if it is to restore its moral credentials. There is, of course, much to be said about the conflict between conservative and liberal approaches on a variety of issues. However, disagreements on these issues are a product of a more fundamental disagreement about moral value. This is not primarily a book about economics, policy, or political strategy, though it has implications for all of these. It is a book about the foundations of morality and how our reigning political ideologies misunderstand those foundations.

PART I

A NATION AT RISK
How Conservatism Is Destroying American Values

As we approach the end of the first decade of the twenty-first century, the United States is at a crossroads. The source of our influence throughout the world has been our moral authority—our commitment to the ideals of freedom, equality, and human welfare. Yet, our moral authority has declined precipitously because of the illegal and immoral war in Iraq, the global recession driven primarily by American economic ideology, an excessively militaristic approach to the threat of terrorism, the use of torture in violation of international norms, and our unwillingness to cooperate with the rest of the world on a variety of environmental, economic, and security issues. Furthermore, our military strength has been sapped by the demands of fighting this unnecessary war and the strategic and tactical mistakes that have squandered time, resources, and human lives.

As the most powerful country and economy in the world, we have a responsibility to use resources wisely and protect the welfare of people affected by our policies. Yet, attempts to slow the proliferation of nuclear weapons throughout the world are failing, thus threatening humanity's survival. Environmental problems such as global warming or the destruction of ocean life pile up one upon the other. But as the world begins to mount a response to these threats, the United States, one of the world's largest polluters, has refused until recently to enter into serious dialogue about environmental problems and lags behind most other developed countries in limiting the environmental impact of its way of life.

Once a nation of immigrants, a beacon of freedom, and a symbol of hope for much of the world, we have allowed the threat of terrorism to make us less welcoming of others. We are fast becoming a nation of closed borders while reverting to an earlier condition of cultural intolerance, where brown people and gay people join African Americans as a subjugated class.

Long suspicious of excessive government power, we now routinely allow electronic surveillance of American citizens and seriously entertain the idea that the president of the United States is a monarch with absolute powers unchecked by Congress or the judiciary. Since our nation's birth, we have stood for the principle that ordinary people matter and should be in control of their lives. Yet corporate power increasingly determines how we live and economic inequality grows exponentially.

Good old American know-how has been the envy of the world. But public goods have received so little sustained, thoughtful attention that our schools are failing, our infrastructure is collapsing, prisons are overflowing, and the healthcare delivery system is dysfunctional. Government agencies from the FDA to the Justice Department have for years been starved for funds, rife with corruption, and ineffective. Finally, the collapse of the housing and credit markets has exposed the lack of appropriate regulatory rules and enforcement mechanisms that could successfully manage a large, complex, and essential American economy.

We are hopeful that the Obama administration will address these issues. But long-term solutions will require an understanding of how we arrived at this sorry condition. Although the causes of these phenomena are complex, the influence of conservatism deserves a significant portion of the blame. When we look back on the Bush administration, it is easy to point fingers at that singular amalgam of dishonesty, incompetence, and hubris. Even many conservatives argue that the administration failed either because it lacked the competence to carry out conservative policies or mistakenly abandoned fundamental conservative principles. But this focus on incompetence and ideological drift is mistaken. The Bush administration, far from being an aberration, carried out the logical consequences of the aspirations of the modern conservative movement. The failures of the Bush administration are the failures of these aspirations and the ideas that animate them.

There is much to say about the failure of conservative policies from Reagan to Bush II, and many books have been written that explain some dimension of our multiple, current crises. But I want to focus on the underlying moral values that made these catastrophes possible. Modern conservatism takes positions on a variety of issues from economics, national security, and constitutional interpretation to the nature of personal happiness, society, and the centrality of religion. Underlying conservative positions on these issues is a particular conception of moral value that drives their positions on the issues and explains the attractions of conservatism. This conservative conception of moral value, which fundamentally misunderstands human nature and the human condition, is responsible for our inability to respond to the various crises our nation faces.

Part 1 describes this mistaken conception of moral value and explains how it contributes to the multiple looming catastrophes that inhibit our flourishing. Chapter 1 describes the moral philosophy of conservatism. Chapters 2, 3, and 4 show that crucial pillars on which this conservatism rests are nonsense. Because I am interested in contemporary conservatism's rise to power, my analysis is focused on conservative thought as articulated by the politicians, activists, and intellectuals who supplied the intellectual capital for that rise to power. I will not be discussing, except in passing, the rich history of conservative thought or the question of whether contemporary conservatism is compatible with its historical antecedents.

philosophy. . . . Man's most sacred possession is his individual soul.[6]

Most of today's conservatives read from the same liturgy of moral failure, crisis, and a rebirth of the soul to be engineered by politicians. Conservatism came to power by trumpeting a comprehensive indictment of contemporary moral values along with proposals for moral improvement that make clear their intention to assemble the troops to battle Beelzebub. According to this indictment, we live in a culture that irresponsibly encourages divorce, single parenthood, and working mothers; a culture of welfare dependency, drug addiction, and family breakdown that inhibits the aspirations of racial minorities and the poor; a popular culture of perverse and offensive messages that subverts all standards of decency by permitting pornography and sexual promiscuity, while endorsing unnatural gay and lesbian lifestyles; a culture ruled by elites who express contempt for American institutions, which are the very foundation, not only of our freedom, but of human freedom in general. We ignore the lawbreakers streaming across our borders, who lack the civilizing influence of American values and refuse to assimilate by learning to speak English. Our respect for human dignity and for life itself wanes as we promote abominations such as abortion, assisted suicide, and embryonic stem-cell research.

Furthermore, conservatives argue, although we have successfully beaten back the menace of communism and have spread our way of life throughout the world, that task was made difficult by an ethos of weakness and complacency that disparages military service and seeks to appease rather than confront external enemies, thus inhibiting our ability to confront new terrorist threats. America, they argue, is an exceptional nation sanctioned by God's plan and destined to bring freedom to the rest of the world. It has a natural, moral superiority when compared to other national traditions. But too many Americans fail to acknowledge this superiority. The soul of America is rotting from within; Satan rides not only with foreign troops but slyly burrows into the hearts and minds of every American undermining the will to resist his entreaties.

Contemporary conservatism has taken on the task of arresting this alleged moral decline. As Pat Buchanan announced at the 1992

Republican Convention, "There is a religious war going on in our country for the soul of America. It is a cultural war, as critical to the kind of nation we will one day be as was the Cold War itself."[7] Religion has always been important in American politics. Contemporary conservatism has ratcheted up that importance by binding the political process to a particular eschatological history. Some conservatives, especially those who focus on economic issues, do not endorse this culture war or buy into the rhetoric about fighting evil. But the conservative movement would not have come to power without it. And, as I will argue shortly, there is an underlying conceptual coherence that binds economic conservatives to the cultural warriors and permits their unholy alliance, despite their disagreements.

According to this conservative narrative, our fall from grace is entangled in the countercultural movements of the 1960s that rejected the solid, working-class virtues of self-discipline, self-reliance, and respect for authority in favor of unrestrained hedonism and self-indulgence, thus eviscerating our sense of personal responsibility. Today, a banal, therapeutic discourse that treats the incompetent as victims of racism, sexism, or economic inequality has replaced the more substantial but unpleasant concepts of guilt and sin, which locate wrongdoing in the individual. Thus, we mistakenly view social ills as products of society that only coercive and expensive government intervention can solve, ignoring the personal, religious transformation required for moral improvement. Moral and spiritual poverty are the root cause of economic failure, not a flawed economic system, as liberals would have us believe. The main impediments to economic success are drug and alcohol abuse, family breakdown, and the absence of a work ethic, issues that require individual moral renewal for their solution.

At bottom, according to this critique, Americans suffer from a pervasive moral weakness that compromises our resistance to inhuman desires. The old liberal forms of social engineering—poverty programs, income redistribution, civil rights legislation, and so on—cannot inoculate us against such temptation and only exacerbate it. Wrongdoing is a personal matter, and transformation comes not through changing social conditions but through changing the self. Thus, the government's role, in collaboration with religious and civic institutions and the free market, is to engineer the transforma-

Thomas Hobbes. Hobbes asserted that human beings are fundamentally selfish, controlled by powerful, unlimited desires prone to shredding any cooperative arrangement the bleeding hearts among us might design. Resources that can satisfy these raging desires are scarce, which inevitably leads to conflict and even more rape and pillaging. Without the moderating influence of civilization, human life would be "nasty, brutish, and short"—total war, 24/7. So if civilized life is to be possible, desires must be restrained.

Hobbes argued that the only way to conceptualize our ability to form communities is to imagine that human beings implicitly agree to a social contract. Each of us must agree to limit our desires as long as we are convinced that others will limit theirs. With this agreement we avoid total war, thus enabling us to satisfy some of our desires. But peace is not yet at hand. Contracts require trust in order to secure the parties' agreement. If I don't believe that other parties to the agreement will hold up their end of the bargain, I have no reason to limit my desires and we are back to the state of total war. What is the basis of the trust needed for the social contract to look like a good deal? Hobbes thought that only a totalitarian political authority, a Leviathan with the power to coerce citizens into honoring the social contract, would guarantee the requisite trust.

Conservatives generally accept Hobbes's view that human desires spiral out of control unless they are reigned in by powerful constraints. However, Hobbes's totalitarian solution is incompatible with liberty and democracy, ideals to which conservatives are at least nominally committed. Thus, conservatives have long argued that liberty is possible only if individuals restrain their own desires. Self-reliance and self-restraint are political as well as personal virtues. When citizens restrain themselves, they do not need excessive government power to keep rampaging desires from disrupting agreements; and when citizens rely on themselves for their sustenance they require fewer agreements that need enforcement. But what motive do we have for becoming such pillars of restraint? If Hobbes is correct about our selfish nature, I should want to acquire as much as I can from others at the least cost to myself, cooperating only when necessary. Why should I wish to persistently limit my desires in order to conform to traditional values? Why should I strive to be self-reliant if I can get a free ride on the resources of others?

If we were utterly selfish, as Hobbes and conservatives claim, then it would seem that no one has a motive for developing self-restraint and self-reliance. Thus, if we are to have a society in which self-restraint and self-reliance are dominant virtues, society will have to be arranged so we are forced to acquire them. Indeed, the conservative political agenda is devoted to developing a social and political culture of sanctions that encourage or coerce individuals to become economically self-sufficient and reign in their desires to conform to traditionally approved activities. Hobbes's totalitarian government is replaced with the soft authoritarianism of normative regulation.

Society must be arranged as a system of "hard knocks" that enforces conformity by exposing individuals to the full consequences of their bad desires. This can occur only if individuals are forced to be self-reliant. The poor should not receive welfare because that would reward and encourage laziness or incompetence; Social Security discourages people from planning adequately for retirement and should be privatized; medical insurance encourages people to request unnecessary healthcare and should be arranged to force people to pay out of pocket; pregnant women should not have the option of abortion and condoms should not be readily available because these encourage irresponsible sex; clean needle programs for addicts are ill advised because they eliminate incentives for stopping drug use; government documents translated into Spanish discourage immigrants from learning English; consumer protection legislation encourages carelessness regarding one's purchases; and permitting same-sex marriage only encourages the deviant behavior. Only when people are exposed to punishment from the bad consequences of their choices, through enforced self-reliance, do they have an incentive to correct their behavior and follow moral absolutes. As is evident from this litany of sanctions, the goal of transforming the moral personality of Americans explains much of the conservative policy agenda on moral values. These sanctions are the mechanisms through which the battle against evil is fought.[9]

If this system of sanctions is to be effective at rebuilding the soul, there must be clear lines of authority that prescribe the limits of possible conduct. Ambiguity about what behavior is expected or who has the authority to enforce sanctions will weaken the message and permit deviations that weaken the will. Thus, institutions organized in hierarchies that depend on the exercise of authority are central to conservative views of how society must function. Religious institutions, the traditional patriarchal family, successful businesses, law enforcement, and the military are worthy of special respect because of the discipline they impose. They constrain the options of individuals through the exercise of authority so that self-restraint and self-reliance do not succumb to the lassitude of uncertainty and are not dissipated across too many choices.[10]

In addition to arming the troops against recalcitrant desire, self-reliance provides conservatism with a criterion by which to judge personal virtue. According to this conservative moral calculus, in a world where every individual is competing for scarce resources, only the strong and self-reliant will be successful. Therefore, material success is the measure of virtue. The unsuccessful lack virtue and deserve their lot because their dependence on others is the result of their lack of discipline and will. Furthermore, the virtuous should have authority over the weak since self-restraint and self-reliance are necessary in combating evil. The distribution of power in society reflects a natural moral order that is the main weapon in the battle against evil. This is one reason why conservatives have been so reluctant to regulate the corruption on Wall Street that caused our recent economic troubles. Wealthy investors were paragons of virtue precisely because they were wealthy and thus could be expected to regulate themselves.

SELF-RELIANCE: THE UNIFYING THEME

The task of building self-reliance and strength of will in the battle against evil is the organizing framework of conservative moral exhortation. Even policies that appear to be based on nonmoral considerations have a moral rationale that rests on self-reliance. Conservative arguments for low taxes and minimal government regulation of business assert that such policies make the economy perform more efficiently. But they also reflect an underlying concern to advance self-reliance as a moral virtue. The oft-repeated slogan that individuals know how to spend their own money better than the government does suggests that businesses and individuals make decisions more conducive to personal happiness when they consult only their own preferences and rely on their own judgments. Furthermore, so the argument goes, we get the appropriate level of consumer and environmental protection only when each individual makes her own decisions on such matters rather than the government. We know ourselves better than others can know us—self-reliance is essential in realizing personal preferences.

Although conservatives insist that unions inhibit the efficiency of labor markets, they also maintain that individual workers are coerced by the demands of union membership and ought to be free to make their own contracts with employers, again extolling self-reliance over collective action in achieving personal goals. Gun ownership should not be regulated for similar reasons—individuals can protect themselves better than government agencies, and at any rate they have a right to supply their own protection if they wish.

Self-reliance is a virtue in foreign affairs as well. If human beings, outside the confines of a nation with the authority to enforce norms, are desire machines devoted to more and more self-aggrandizement, then the world of foreign affairs will be a war of all against all. Because there is no political authority to enforce international agreements and encourage trust, there can be no moral relationship between states. Thus, external evils are a constant threat, appeasement always a fool's errand, and cooperation at best a temporary expedient. When interests conflict, nothing secures cooperation except the exercise of power and the use of force. The capability for unilateral military action is essential for the battle against evil. Military solutions to global conflict are attractive because they enable us to take matters into our own hands, instead of relying on treaties and agreements that may restrict our ability to defend ourselves.

As these examples demonstrate, the entire agenda of modern conservatism is a paean to self-reliance and strength of will as a bulwark against iniquity. Conservatism is not a monolithic belief system and conservatives differ on moral issues such as abortion, immigration, gay rights, and welfare. Many will disavow the rhetoric of the battle against evil. However, despite these disagreements, there is an underlying continuity to conservative thought regarding values that is centered on the concept of a person who possesses self-reliance. This soul-building agenda and the vision of the person that supports it ties together the disparate elements that make up the conservative coalition.

Today, religious conservatives, both Catholic and Protestant, are the most vocal and active proponents of social conservatism. They are united in their acceptance of the moral authority of conservative understandings of religious tradition; in promoting the so-called "culture of life" that opposes abortion, embryonic stem-cell research, and euthanasia; in their opposition to gay and lesbian initiatives; and in striving to undermine the separation of church and state. It should be said that Catholics tend to be less enthusiastic than Protestants about the virtues of the free market.

LIBERTARIAN CONSERVATIVES

Coalition politics requires unholy alliances. Although conservative libertarians and social conservatives tend to affiliate with the Republican Party and vote for the same candidates, they often disagree profoundly on questions of moral value. While social conservatives lament the absence of constraints on our conduct, libertarians insist there are so many constraints that our fundamental interest in liberty is threatened.

Liberty—our entitlement to collective rights guaranteeing our freedom—is the dominant value for libertarians. The government's proper role is solely to protect our interest in making our own choices. Thus, the protection of private property is the essential function of government. Fire and police protection, a legal structure to enforce contracts, the defense of civil liberties, and provisions to defend borders are legitimate uses of public resources. Beyond these minimal functions, government should not restrict our activity or impose burdens or obligations. Thus, libertarians will not endorse government-sponsored coercion on moral issues, which they view as illegitimate meddling in private affairs.

The political alliance between social conservatives and libertarians is cemented by their shared antipathy toward the welfare state, the level of taxation required to sustain it, and the loss of individual responsibility in a society organized around centralized, bureaucratic institutions. Social conservatives hate these features of modern life because they inhibit the development of self-reliance and self-restraint required to be moral beings. Libertarians hate these features of modern life because they inhibit the development of self-reliance required to be genuinely free. Liberty is available only to the self-reliant person who is free because she is not dependent on others and promotes freedom for others as well because she requires very little from them. The common denominator that cements this coalition is their shared vision of an ideal person—one who possesses the virtue of self-reliance.

NEOCONSERVATISM

Neoconservatism is a movement initiated in the 1970s by former liberals who were disenchanted with government spending on poverty programs and the failure of many liberals during the Cold War to take a strong stand against communism. Unlike social conservatives or libertarians, neoconservatives do not object in principle to government solutions to domestic problems. They often adopt much of the rhetoric of liberals regarding the importance of alleviating poverty, ending racism, and promoting equality. However, they are skeptical about whether government programs achieve these goals and prefer to rely on allegedly more efficient private organizations, free markets, and individual initiative to achieve them. Like social conservatives and libertarians, neoconservatives advocate self-reliance because it allegedly strengthens individuals in ways that make equality and prosperity available to everyone. Like social conservatives, most neoconservatives view traditions as the source of moral standards and view the United States as engaged in a historical battle against evil.

Neoconservatives have had their greatest influence on foreign policy by reshaping traditional conservative foreign policy postures. Throughout much of the twentieth century, conservatives and libertarians advocated isolationist or realist foreign policies that supported national self-reliance. They believed that treaties and alliances with other countries pull us into conflicts in which we have no compelling interest. Thus, alliances should be avoided and military force employed only when it advances our interests and should never be used to promote a moral agenda, advance humanitarian concerns, or to engage in nation building.

In opposition to traditional foreign policy conservatism, neoconservatives contend it is in our national interest to use our military might to advance freedom and democracy throughout the world. In the battle against evil, the best hopes for humanity are carried by American ideals, for American traditions, with our commitment to freedom, capitalism, and democracy, express human aspirations. America is the exception; the only hope that evil can be defeated. This is especially true in the Middle East where, neoconservatives argue, the cause of democracy, rights for women, and religious liberties can be advanced only through military action. In this enterprise, neoconservatives are often joined by religious conservatives who find these hopes expressed in the eschatology of the Bible. But this is nevertheless to be accomplished without excessive input or interference from other nations. In contrast to their isolationist past, conservatives now grudgingly admit that our nation's welfare is affected by the welfare of other nations, but our interventions must be self-directed affairs. Self-reliance remains a virtue because only our traditions are up to the task of battling evil.

PRO-BUSINESS CONSERVATISM

The final constituency that makes up modern conservatism is pro-business conservatism. Pro-business conservatives believe the welfare of the nation, especially with regard to the availability of jobs, the pace of economic growth, and economic competitiveness, is dependent on the welfare of business organizations. Profits "trickle down" to other social agents so that the common good is served through increasing profit margins. Thus, the power of government should be used to promote business interests through tax cuts, direct subsidies, minimal regulation, and access to government policy-making agencies. We might call this the "lobbyist as hero" agenda.

Pro-business conservatism is politically allied with the other varieties of conservatism because of its support for low tax rates and minimal government regulation. Pro-business conservatives are less interested in the moral issues that animate social conservatism and often find themselves at odds with libertarians over the appropriateness of government subsidies of business. Laws that permit tax shelters, a dizzying array of tax credits, and regulations that favor business interests, not to mention direct injections of capital (recently dubbed "bailouts"), are among the many ways in which government subsidizes business. Nevertheless, the dominance of self-reliance as a virtue appeals to pro-business conservatives, despite their appetite for government handouts, because it supports the ethos of individualism that encourages workers and consumers to see themselves as self-reliant individuals rather than as members of collective interest groups who might challenge the scope of corporate power. When labor unions are weak and consumers disorganized, corporate power is enhanced. More important, the traditions of American Exceptionalism support the export of American life including the products of corporate capitalism, which enhances corporate profits, enriches military and defense industries, and provides moral authority to attempts by American corporations to control the world's resources.

In summary, all four components of the conservative coalition, despite substantial disagreement on a variety of issues, endorse the ideal of a person in which self-reliance is the dominant virtue and tradition the primary source of moral authority. Thus, all varieties of conservatism endorse the soul-shaping agenda. This concept of a traditional, self-reliant person is what attracts voters to conservatism. Conservative voters see themselves as self-reliant and support political agendas that appear to promise a society committed to self-reliance, which is a plausible way of life only when pursued against a background of strong moral authority vested in religious and national traditions.

WHY CONSERVATISM ATTRACTS VOTERS

To most liberals, the success of the conservative moral agenda is puzzling. Rather than providing real solutions to problems, it seems to rest on intolerance, greed, and an authoritarian need to control people's lives. Thus, we explain away its attraction as a symptom of voter ignorance or their cynical manipulation by conservative elites. But this is a mistake. There is logic in the support enjoyed by the conservative agenda, although it is based on implausible and dangerous premises—it is vital that we grasp this logic.

In recent decades, many people have felt that they are not keeping up with the changes that roil their communities. People who believe that control over one's life requires only self-discipline, hard work, and delayed gratification—the products of a strong will—are disheartened to find that, in this hypercompetitive society, skills, knowledge, ambition, and information are more important. This marks a class distinction between an educated elite at the cutting edge of culture and large numbers of undereducated people who face uncertain prospects and little social status, despite their willingness to work hard and play by the rules. As new technology increases productivity, communications between elites throughout the world improves, and cheap labor markets overseas reduce the demand for labor, it is becoming increasingly clear that the "little guy" is no longer the ballast that keeps our economy and culture afloat. This lack of status breeds fear and powerful longings for the old values to make a comeback.

Furthermore, the emergence of alternative lifestyles, changes in norms governing race relations and gender, and the impact of immigration in previously homogeneous neighborhoods water down the authority of some American traditions, making them seem optional rather than necessary ingredients in a good life. Cultural change is rapid, pervasive, and deep—what it means to be a man, a woman, or an American are contested and up for grabs. As a consequence, many people perceive their traditional local culture—a system of community norms, patterns of social interaction, and a conception of the kinds of activities and attitudes that constitute living a good life— fading in importance as well as in substance. When rural, small-town America dies, a way of life dies with it. People can rebuild their economic prospects, but they can retrieve culture only in memory. The loss of culture is one of the most profound losses we can suffer because fundamental questions about how to live no longer have clear answers.

As a result, many parents worry that their kids, largely unsupervised because of crushing work schedules, are learning too much from the toxins that ooze from computers and televisions, and worry that they have no reliable way of transmitting cultural meanings to their children. Thus, they find that the moral absolutes and community activities of religion provide a sense of security and clarity lacking in the larger society. Although voters worry about their ability to prosper economically, the erosion of culture is a significant threat as well.

The future may be interesting but it looks anything but secure and, for many people, it doesn't look like it belongs to them. It is not surprising that in the face of massive cultural change some people begin to see their traditional way of life as bound up in a metaphysical battle between good and evil. Worries about the erosion of culture dovetail with traditional Christian themes of an epic struggle in which the person is the battleground on which the fate of the world rests and the transformation of souls becomes the task of civilization and the Republican Party.

In contrast to global economic and technological forces that are out of the control of individuals, cultural decline appears to have definite and assignable causes. Gay marriage, illegal immigration, teenage pregnancy, abortion, gun ownership, and religious belief are about the personal decisions that people make. They are, apparently, not under the control of distant corporations, impersonal market forces, or foreign fanatics but are within the purview of schools, churches, parents and their kids, and local businesses and politicians. In this arena, self-discipline, delayed gratification, and playing by the rules can make a difference in reversing this perceived cultural decline. Granted, the destructive forces of capitalism contribute to cultural erosion and uncertainty—the mobility of money, people, and goods is the most significant cause of community fragmentation and cultural change. But since these forces are beyond the control of individuals, many voters focus on the moral issues that seem to be within their control. Pour into this cultural turmoil the threat of terrorism and we have a cauldron of fear and anxiety stirred and spiced by right-wing politicians and media seeking an advantage for their favorite cause.

Why does conservatism offer a compelling framework for understanding and responding to these anxieties? In the face of uncertainty, people tend to focus on what they can control by latching onto fixed ideas that provide the most structure to their lives and maintain clear lines of authority. Conservatism is able to market itself as the solution to this uncertainty.

Conservative ideology promotes self-reliance and the power of locally controlled institutions to advance welfare. It insists that individuals should be able to hold onto and control their money and make their own decisions about their needs. It is skeptical that ordinary people can benefit from government redistribution. It argues

Religion is too deeply influenced by capitalism to be an effective form of resistance to the world of self-gratification and consumption. To satisfy our material needs we must live in "McWorld," which appropriates and reformulates as a marketing device any fugitive idea that might survive from our spiritual quest. So, today, for many, religion is just another lifestyle choice marketed by self-help gurus who urge us to think positively so we can sell more insurance and celebrate with athletes who assure us that God hits home runs. The aim of much modern religion is to achieve secular success, with a little help from my omnipotent friend—steroids without the side effects. Self-denial, the lynchpin of the old Protestant ethic, if it were to sweep America, would cause demand for goods to plummet, thereby threatening the economic growth that is the very basis of American capitalism. So the lion will inevitably have the lamb for lunch. The best the lamb can hope for is to enjoy being eaten. The cheerleading of the religious Right for any half-baked, free market idea shows that there is no real resistance here.

Given the difficulty of integrating religious and consumerist values, the path of least resistance for many people is to create two worlds—one for Mammon, one for God—and take care that they do not interpenetrate. Religion becomes a private matter pursued for its metaphysical comfort, having little to do with the messy conduct of everyday life. This is a promising approach for a functioning democracy, since it protects the political process from the combustible mixture of religious and political passion. Unfortunately, such a détente has not satisfied those religious authorities hungering for political power, who recognize that the losses suffered when the sacred becomes incoherent can be ignored when the sanctified get rich. As a result, an increasingly common approach among the faithful is to count the cash and hit the mall before retreating to tribal loyalties, assembling rhetorical bombs to hurl at the bloodless mechanical beast that feeds us. Hence, fundamentalisms are born eschewing charity, forgiveness, and peace in favor of ritual displays of manly fortitude—the ultimate pose for conservatives. In a reality framed by Hollywood, if you can't actually be a Christian, the next best thing is to play one in a tragicomedy where the spectacle of Bibles, bigotry, and bling might at least entertain God, who surely is an ironist.

If the refuge for exhausted revelers is not modern "cafeteria" religion, conservatives will insist that only traditional, fundamentalist religion can still the pulse of desirous hearts. Here, where doubt, uncertainty, and ambivalence are ruled out of court, all of the aforementioned conflicts between religion and capitalism can be wiped away by self-deception, which is all that sustains this unholy alliance.

THE "AUTHORITY" OF TRADITIONS

Our religious traditions cannot effectively manage the overproduction of desire in modern consumer societies. But traditional values, when they have absolute authority, bring about an even more profound calamity—they weaken our moral capacities.

In the conservative moral imagination, traditions are unambiguous, authoritative guides for how we should live, and judgments about right and wrong are correct only if they conform to well-established conventions. But which traditions should have authority? Conservatives have special regard for the traditions of Christianity and American Exceptionalism. We must honor and sustain the traditional family structure, allegedly dictated by the Gospels, which must consist of a heterosexual, breadwinning father in authority and a heterosexual mother who takes care of the children and the home and defers to her husband on important matters. We must oppose abortion, respect authority, respect private property and the freedom to use it as one sees fit, work hard to support ourselves, and endorse the moral superiority of the United States, its leaders, and its impact on world affairs. These are values that have been embraced by most Americans since the founding of the nation and are sanctioned by God. They are alleged to be the source of our strength and the reason for our success. According to conservatives, these traditions represent moral absolutes that cannot be compromised or weakened if we are to remain strong—dissent cannot be tolerated.[2]

But what gives these particular traditions their special authority? We do not live in a nation where only one tradition or one interpretation of a tradition is available. In modern, pluralistic democracies, citizens represent many ethnic, cultural, religious, or moral traditions, which give conflicting prescriptions regarding how to live, how to treat others, and what is permissible or forbidden.

Government must make decisions about which traditions are to be legally protected and financially supported. When government chooses one tradition over another as a basis for public policy, participants in the tradition not chosen may be marginalized or subordinated. Government cannot be neutral between competing traditions because decisions about policy inevitably enhance the prospects of some traditions and discourage the prospects of others. For instance, the traditions of Christianity have exerted enormous influence over our legal and moral norms in the United States, but equally strong is the influence of our traditions of freedom of conscience and the separation of church and state. These two important traditions clash when, for example, conservative Christians argue that gay marriage ought to be banned because homosexuality is forbidden according to their interpretation of the Bible.

Adherents of the tradition that loses this debate will surely be harmed, coerced by law into accepting something they find unacceptable. This coercion is not necessarily objectionable. Governments, by their nature, coerce citizens to follow the law. But in a democracy, the coercion must have a good reason, one that the coerced citizens would themselves see as a reason, albeit one with which they may disagree. In other words, in a democracy, public reasons must appeal to all of us as *reasons* rather than arbitrary impositions of power. However, if conservative Christians succeed in banning gay marriage, it will seem unprincipled to supporters of gay marriage—an exercise of naked power on the part of a powerful interest group. If proponents of gay marriage prevail it will seem to conservative Christians like an unprincipled capitulation to the "gay rights agenda"—an exercise of naked power on the part of a powerful interest group. Appealing to "our traditions" won't confer legitimacy on the decision since the contending traditions are both ours.

A fair solution seems possible only if there are criteria for deciding such issues that have some independence from the traditions in conflict. For instance, we may decide the issue based on empirical evidence regarding the effects of the respective policies on the institution of marriage, or data on whether gay and lesbian folks can be effective parents. But to accept such a rationale is to adopt a standard that has standing independently of the traditions in conflict. If we adopt this independent standard, the moral authority for the policy is not tradition but some other consideration—in this case empirical evidence regarding marriage practices. Resolutions of divisive issues such as gay marriage will have legitimacy only if traditions are not viewed as having absolute authority.

The fact remains that we are a pluralistic nation made up of many competing traditions, all of which count as "ours," and if we are to survive as a nation we must find some way of making decisions that do not exclude large segments of our population from full participation. How we are to accomplish this is a difficult question, but insisting on the absolute moral authority of tradition will not answer it.

Despite the importance of traditions, they cannot do the work that conservatives wish them to do. Modern pluralistic democracies must solve the problem of how to get diverse people to live together peacefully. Conservatives who endorse the authority of tradition have no solution to this problem and thus face a dilemma. Either there is a higher standard that governs our political choices regarding which traditions to support, or there is not. If there is no higher standard, then we have no rational basis for deciding which of the many competing traditions should be the basis of public policy. What is right will simply depend on who has the power to push his or her agenda. But that leads directly to relativism—questions of right and wrong are relative to the group with the most political power. If there is a higher standard by which we can judge competing traditions, then we should base our policies on the tradition that best meets that higher standard. But then it isn't the tradition that has ultimate authority but the higher standard to which we are appealing. Thus, conservatives must give up the claim that traditions are the ultimate moral authority or embrace relativism, which they argue is the cause of our moral decline. Conservative diatribes against "liberal relativism" are just self-deceptive blather. In endorsing the absolute authority of traditions, conservatives must embrace relativism, because what is right or wrong is relative to some preferred tradition that is far from universal and for which they can offer no further defense. Thus, the first way in which appeals to tradition undermine our moral capacities is that they sap our ability to resolve moral disagreement.

ditions and enforced by authority, as conservatives would have it. Instead, moral development requires the development of a capacity for independent thinking and the careful balancing of a variety of competing considerations. The ability to stand back from our habits and reflect on them, the moment of doubt to which I referred above, is essential for developing moral capacities.

Turiel's results are not limited to children; he draws similar conclusions about adults from a variety of cross-cultural surveys. Even in cultures alleged to be traditional, the authority-independent character of moral judgments is apparent. The conservative view that morality is authority dependent is not supported by psychological research.

AUTHORITARIANISM AND AMERICAN VALUES

The consequences of a highly influential ideology ignoring basic facts about morality are predictable and disturbing. We would expect a political morality that justifies moral claims by appeal to institutionalized authority to be comfortable with vast inequalities of social power, since it is through unequal authority relations that moral norms are enforced. But insouciance toward equality is not the worst of it. Authoritarianism also encourages individuals to abdicate their sense of personal responsibility and defer to authorities, leading to a fatal moral blindness.

Widespread public acceptance of the Iraq War provides ample evidence of a troubling authoritarianism that saps us of our moral capacities. The run up to the war witnessed a conservative movement, the public, and a press corps uncritically accepting patently false and fantastic claims made by the Bush administration about threats posed by Iraq and the ease of establishing a client state in the troubled region of the Middle East. After it became clear that there was no security threat that justified the war, most Americans dutifully ignored the cost in lives as they continued to support the war effort. The prolonged war also revealed a public willing to accept the claims of the Bush administration to be above the law in its use of domestic surveillance and treatment of prisoners. Politicians in power are prone to this sort of abuse. That the public and the press largely acquiesced indicates the degree to which deference to institutionalized authority has permeated our culture. This troubling deference to authority is not confined to war. Calls by religious conservatives for government policy to strictly adhere to religious doctrines are nothing but an attempt to impose an authoritarian hierarchy on a liberal democracy. The use of religious and moral language to promote an economic agenda designed to further enrich the already wealthy implicitly endorses the authoritarian idea that the powerful must be good because moral goodness is the will of the powerful. Only such a conception could explain how felons such as Jack Abramoff, Duke Cunningham, and Tom DeLay, the poster boys for the Bush corruption era, could believe their corrupt activities were doing God's work.[6]

The habit of confusing conventional, authority-dependent judgments with moral requirements continues to distort debates about values in this country. Most conservatives insist on traditional gender roles and family structure; most are opposed to birth control, abortion, and gay rights, environmental and consumer regulations, social services for the poor, and Social Security programs; and they demand that only English be spoken, that undocumented immigrants be treated as criminals, and that the United States has the right to invade any country we wish for any reason we deem sufficient. Each of these policies is accompanied by a studied indifference to the harm they would produce. Each is advanced by arguments that some long-standing tradition is under threat and must be rescued.

As Turiel shows, this is not the soil in which a moral conscience can grow. Only when society focuses on fairness, justice, and vulnerability can citizens develop and sustain a moral conscience and accept personal responsibility for their actions. Excessive deference to authority and respect for tradition conceal the harm that our actions cause and prevent us from securing a moral basis for our social relations.

This is why appeals to tradition cannot respond to the problem of the overproduction of desire, the discussion that opened this chapter. The moral blindness of authoritarianism is complicit in the expansion of desire. When we defer to institutionalized authority in moral matters, we are less inclined to take personal responsibility for our own judgments and lack the perceptiveness that can keep up with the constantly roiling moral waters of contemporary capitalism. The decline in morality that conservatives lament is the product of the very policies they endorse.

result of deliberate policies advanced by conservative cheerleaders with bromides about allegedly free enterprise and the free market.[8]

THE REFORM BOONDOGGLE

According to the conservative "soul-shaping" agenda, the poor are not the only ones who need moral improvement. The aged, the ill, and the young could use some bucking up as well. Our healthcare delivery system, schools, and entitlement programs need reform, and conservatives have hustled their self-reliance regime to the top of the reform agenda. Conservatives have argued that healthcare would be more efficiently distributed if people were forced to pay for their own care rather than rely on insurance.[9] Allegedly, people are willing to waste the insurance company's money on unnecessary medical care but would not so readily waste their own. If they had to pay for healthcare out of pocket, or out of their own health savings account, they would more carefully scrutinize their real need for medical care before purchasing it. The idea is to make health outcomes depend on a person's choices—we live or die as self-reliant individuals.

This proposal understands healthcare as a kind of free good once insurance gets into the picture. It assumes that we want more healthcare than we actually need—those evil infinite desires once again threaten to get out of control. Insurance feeds the ravenous beast by insulating us from the consequences of wanting too much healthcare since the cost of an individual's insurance policy is not dependent on how often that individual makes a claim. If we force people to weigh the real cost of a trip to the doctor, they would go only when necessary. Once again, in theory, shifting risk onto individuals sharpens the mind and the will.

But is this an even remotely plausible account of the real incentives in the purchase of healthcare? Of course, with regard to some products we might consume more if there were a ceiling beyond which we didn't have to pay for more product. Subsidize beer consumption after work and people will probably drink more beer. But healthcare and beer are dissimilar commodities. Although, even among beer lovers, there are limits to how much beer they want, all things being equal most beer lovers prefer more beer to less. Such is not the case with healthcare. Most wealthy people who can afford it do not check into the hospital on a whim. For most of us, getting medical treatment is unpleasant and time consuming and we only seek it out when we need it.

More important, as any healthcare professional knows, people tend to ignore symptoms as often as they exaggerate them. The average person is incapable of distinguishing between necessary and unnecessary visits to the doctor since he lacks the medical knowledge to accurately interpret symptoms. In the absence of any well-confirmed belief about their symptoms, many people ignore them at their peril. Forcing people to pay out of their own pocket provides them with an additional, very powerful incentive to put off going to the doctor, leading to more expensive, negative outcomes later on.

Exposing people to the consequences of their ill-informed actions will not lead to wiser choices and will not encourage patients to take more personal responsibility for their health. In the absence of adequate health insurance, people must make difficult trade-offs between healthcare and other goods without the information required to make a good decision. The outcome of such a policy is not self-reliance but fear and trembling. Whether one chooses well is a matter of luck. A society based on this simulacrum of self-reliance is a fortune-cookie society in which individuals must passively wait to see if they are crushed or liberated by their dimly understood "choices."

Conservative education policy is another arena in which the road to self-reliant virtue sends us plunging into an abyss. Conservatives have promoted (and liberals have acquiesced to) standardized testing and measurement regimes in public schools that require schools and individual students to reach government-mandated benchmarks each year. The successful schools are rewarded with more funding; the unsuccessful schools will see their funding decline if they do not improve. These tests often determine whether students graduate or advance in grade level, and many conservatives want teacher performance evaluated using these tests and think parents should use test results to decide which school their child should attend. President Bush's No Child Left Behind Act is one example of how this general approach has been implemented in the third and fourth grades.

The idea behind these policies is that competition to improve scores and the imposition of sanctions when benchmarks are not met will motivate teachers and school officials to work harder and smarter in order to educate children, instead of relying on government funding to improve outcomes. This will make students, teachers, and school officials personally responsible for the outcome of their actions. They will come to see outcomes as flowing from their own desires, beliefs, and effort, from their individual choices, rather than blaming poor performance on inadequate funding or social inequalities.

Once again, the expectation that competition and coercive sanctions will lead to greater personal responsibility is mistaken. As a result of these policies, we can expect teachers, school officials, and students to adopt a variety of strategies to increase their chances of competing successfully. The most common is to devote extensive class time to test-taking strategies, covering only materials that are likely to show up on the test, or aligning curriculum to conform too narrowly to objectives set by state bureaucracies or textbook publishers, leaving out of the curriculum content and skills that are not tested. The less competent the teacher, the more incentive she has to adopt such a strategy. The depth and breadth of education suffers as a result. Teachers will restrict curriculum, will be less able to respond to students' interests, and the pace of instruction will conform to test schedules rather than students' learning capacities. Because teachers are pitted against each other in a competition that may ultimately determine salary and job security, teachers no longer have incentives to cooperate, inhibiting the sharing of information and exacerbating management problems within schools.[10]

Furthermore, because students differ in their abilities, some students will struggle to pass these exams and will withdraw their efforts in order to protect self-esteem. The prospect of failure is seldom an effective motivational tool, if the chances of success are slim. An increased dropout rate is a likely consequence of high-stakes testing.

The most disturbing result is that even good students are less likely to acquire a love of learning for its own sake when coerced to view high test scores as the aim of education; and teachers have less time and inclination to instill a love of learning in students because the incentives require that they focus on test scores. The survivors may succeed in generating high test scores, but students will know they have not learned much of value and teachers will know they have not taught much, and neither will see the outcome as their responsibility since the system imposes an aim that is extrinsic to the practice in which they are engaged. The aim of education is learning and skill building, not high test scores, which reflect only a portion of what students learn.

The attempt to use coercive sanctions and competition to encourage students and teachers to accept responsibility for their performance produces only cynicism. Even when teachers and students successfully compete, they will not see their actions flowing from their core motivational states, which are connected to teaching and learning, not test scores. Under such circumstances, the common human tendency is to disavow the actual motive as "not really me." The result of this approach to education reform is likely to be poorly educated students, less-motivated teachers, and less willingness on the part of either to accept responsibility for the outcome. Strength of will might be enhanced among those who enjoy the competition, but it is not directed toward the appropriate end.

The conclusion to draw from all of this is that when incentives distort the goal structure of an activity by replacing intrinsically valued aims—such as education or good health—with goals that are only indirectly or instrumentally related to an activity, such as high test scores or profit, people seldom accept full responsibility for the consequences of their actions since their actions do not reflect their core motives. Doctors concerned primarily with the bottom line are not better doctors, parents forced to work longer hours to support their families are not better parents, government officials concerned with staying in power rather than providing service are not better officials—in each case their motivations have been corrupted. Teachers and students are no different in this regard.

Similar misguided attempts to produce self-reliant individuals underlie almost all conservative policy proposals. In each case, they ignore the capacities that enable genuinely self-reliant persons. If conservatives had their way, legislation that protects consumers from faulty products and allows consumers to sue if they have been harmed would be sharply curtailed.[11] The aim is to make consumers take more responsibility for their purchases rather than relying on lawsuits or government regulation to protect them from unscrupulous actors. But such a policy would not produce self-reliant consumers. Consumers often lack the information needed to make genuinely informed decisions, and even when the information is available the cost of acquiring that information is high. Most of the time, there is no way to find out if a product is defective until after the purchase. In the absence of consumer protections, rather than taking more responsibility for their purchases, rational consumers would recognize they are powerless to control the outcome of purchases and withdraw from the market as much as possible. Less rational consumers will simply leave matters to fortune and make haphazard purchases, hoping today is their lucky day.

Similarly, conservatives assume that if women were prevented from having abortions they would become less sexually active since they would be unable to use abortion to avoid the consequences of sexual activity. But there is ample evidence that, in the absence of legal abortions, women seek back-alley abortions or more modern chemical abortions.[12] Some women, if they are assertive enough and have power within their relationships, may insist that their partners use condoms, but many women are not in a situation to make such demands. When caught between the imperatives of sexual desire and the inability to have an abortion, they will likely see themselves as powerless against forces they cannot control. Rather than withdraw from the activity, they will engage in it haphazardly. After all, if they had it together enough to use birth control, they would be doing so already.

Coercive sanctions and threats do not encourage personal responsibility because the person being coerced views them as an external force that is independent of her will. They seldom succeed in getting people to internalize a moral judgment that they have not come to themselves. Laws against all variety of activities—prohibition, drug laws, prostitution, illegal immigration, gambling, forms of communication we dislike—drive the activity underground rather than eliminate it. The law and other coercive measures will force changes in behavior but are less successful at dissecting moral motivation and repairing it. Repair occurs only by aligning the goals of individuals with the goals of the community through interpersonal dialogue, empathy, compassion, and caring activity. The moral experience of individuals shows much more variability and nuance than the crude, uninformed judgments of government bureaucrats, hustlers looking to make a buck, and the police. Human beings do not respond to the stick with the proper attitude unless there are a variety of carefully arranged carrots to provide purpose and direction. But the tools in the conservative arsenal—competition, risk, and coercive threat—are far too crude to provide genuine incentives.[13]

Just to be clear, I am not arguing that competition is always a poor motivator or that coercive sanctions never work. Competition is an effective motivator when there is a clear metric that determines winners and losers and that metric is part of the goal structure of the activity in question, as in athletic competitions and business transactions. In athletic competitions, the goal is to win, and metrics such as points scored or elapsed time determine unambiguously the winner. In business transactions, the goal is to maximize profit, which can be precisely measured in terms of dollars, share price, asset values, and so on. But in activities in which the ultimate goal is not victory over an opponent or when there is no clear metric for determining victory, competition distorts the goal structure of the activity.

Similarly, coercive sanctions are effective when behavior must be modified without regard for the beliefs of the person being sanctioned. Even the threat of incarceration, though effective at deterring crime, typically does not effect the moral beliefs of the criminal. Coercive sanctions, without some additional mechanism for encouraging appropriate beliefs, will encourage neither personal responsibility nor self-reliance. Coercion, exposure to risk, and competition may modify behavior—they are less effective in shaping souls.

There is no evidence that this grand conservative experiment in social engineering is succeeding. Which social practice has improved over the past thirty years of conservative hegemony except the practice of making money? The work of civilization—healthcare delivery, education, care for the indigent, care for the environment, solving coordination and cooperation problems, discouraging criminal activity without costly and destructive incarceration, managing international conflict—has suffered while we conduct a dangerous experiment in moral motivation. Only the pursuit of technical knowledge has kept pace because in an information society, such knowledge has a price. But it is not at all clear that civilization can rest only on technique. When self-reliance is encouraged without a sense of moral responsibility, the result is at best an individual without the intrinsic motivations that enable us to improve our social practices; at worst it produces an ugly, narcissistic individual who seeks only personal aggrandizement.

TRUST AND THE CORRUPTION OF SELF-RELIANCE

I have been arguing that conservative policies designed to build self-reliance fail because they distort motives and ignore the elements of moral psychology that make self-reliance possible. But this experiment in social engineering has a more global effect that threatens the very fabric of society. Conservative policies and values undermine the most precious commodity for any society—social trust—because they confuse the virtue of self-reliance with its corrupt cousin, the goal of self-sufficiency.

Trust is essential because human beings are vulnerable to a variety of physical and psychic harms that we cannot prevent by acting as individuals. We are especially dependent on the forbearance, if not the kindness, of strangers. Each of us depends on a system of mutual assurances, so that whenever we encounter another person we are reasonably sure he intends no serious harm. A minimal level of social trust is necessary for even the most casual or perfunctory relationship. Thus, each of us has an incentive to be trustworthy and to insist on the trustworthiness of others. If I am not trustworthy, or give the appearance of being untrustworthy, I make myself vulnerable since I cannot depend on the mutual assurances that people would otherwise extend to me, which closes off the benefits of social cooperation. Thus, my own trustworthiness makes sense to me only if I see myself as dependent on others. If I view myself as a self-sufficient individual with no need to depend on others, I have no incentive to be trustworthy or to regard trust as an important social good.

Self-reliance, properly understood, enhances social trust because the self-reliant person does not impose excessive burdens on others. But self-reliance is a virtue that, like other virtues, can be excessive or deficient. As the Greek philosopher Aristotle argued, being virtuous is a matter of hitting the mean between two extremes. A genuinely self-reliant person is neither too dependent nor too independent of others. She recognizes when she can and when she cannot rely on her own resources and capabilities. But excessive self-reliance is as dangerous as too little self-reliance because it easily mutates into the vice of self-sufficiency, which fails to acknowledge the fundamental fact that we are utterly dependent on others for our existence and flourishing.[14]

The pursuit of self-sufficiency inhibits trust because it aims at a kind of invulnerability that obviates the need to be trustworthy. The self-sufficient person strives to live without depending on others. But that means relieving herself of the burdens of the system of assurances on which we all depend. The more invulnerable and self-sufficient I make myself, the less I need worry about whether others are trustworthy or consider me trustworthy. This severs the mutual assurances that make social life possible. Fight or flight is the only rational response to an encounter with someone who is indifferent to matters of trust. Society needs self-reliant persons who can recognize when the claims they make on others are unreasonable or damaging, but this cannot come at the expense of a deeper recognition of our dependence on each other that requires trust.

The quickest route to holding this noxious belief that one is self-sufficient is to take advantage of differences in social power, wealth, and prestige. The more power and wealth I have, the less I need be concerned with the system of social cooperation that the less powerful depend on. This is one reason why extreme social and economic inequalities are dangerous for any society—they isolate people from the consequences of defecting from the system of social cooperation that supports social trust. In other words, the social conditions of morality require conditions of rough equality. Without rough equality, those with social power, relatively unconstrained by the demands of others, can more easily convince themselves of their invulnerability and run roughshod over any conception of moral value. Hence the platitude that power corrupts.

Conservative policies and values promote vast inequalities of wealth that invite successful individuals to see themselves as self-sufficient and inspire everyone else to aspire to self-sufficiency as well.[15] Lifted from the pages of Ayn Rand, the quest to become an absolutely sovereign individual answerable to no one becomes a personal ideal. The attitudes encouraged by this socially sanctioned autism send the message that life is fundamentally about competition, not the pursuit of happiness or self-fulfillment. In this competition, we are discouraged from relying on government or government-supported institutions. Thus, democratic politics and institutions become less central to our lives and the idea of citizenship loses its meaning. In the absence of a coherent idea of citizenship, the institutions of civil society—churches, schools, clubs, and so on—along with a variety of personal and family relationships may become more important to us as we try to maintain a grip on social life. However, because the aim of life is victory, or survival if victory is out of reach, our commitment to these institutions and relationships is contingent on their serving our narrow, selfish purposes rather than the goals of the institution or relationship. Corruption becomes the new normal, and conflict dominates most interactions. People withdraw and social solidarity wanes. We succeed by taking what we can get and escaping before the consequences come due.[16]

With fewer shared beliefs and increasing conflicts between individual interests, moralistic rage at anyone who poses an obstacle becomes the dominant public stance and fear of strangers or outsiders the primary means of coping. A willingness to take risks becomes a virtue as we try to find some way of gaining an advantage—thrill seeking becomes the badge of character, consumption the way in which we keep score. And many simply fall by the wayside because they can't compete—modern lepers because they remind us of where we might end up if we falter.

Such is the life conservatives would have us lead. If we are not living such lives yet, it is because the conscience resists, though we may be too preoccupied with shopping to notice. This culture of corruption is evident in the accounting scandals and investment high jinks that have ruined the US economy, in the rivers of cash that bribe politicians to favor special interests that harm the public, and in the politicization of every agency of government carried out by the Bush administration. There are disturbing signs that the rest of us are increasingly coming to resemble these government and business elites. From journalists who plagiarize or misrepresent their credentials, athletes who take performance-enhancing drugs, doctors who allow kickbacks from drug companies to influence decisions about prescriptions, to churches that are little more than cash machines preying on desperate people, we are increasingly coming to resemble the folks at Enron. The United States remains a vibrant nation held together by strong moral traditions. But the huckster has always been an American icon of sorts eliciting a grudging admiration when the "con" is especially delicious. If we have come to believe in our absolute sovereignty, we can all be content with the delusion that we are in on the "con," hucksters with a good conscience. It is not at all surprising that our current economic crisis was caused by the corruption of some of our most respected financial institutions and the allegedly "wise" men and women who led them.

The excessive pursuit of self-sufficiency not only isolates the well off from the consequences of their actions—it also disables the motivation of the less well off to buy into the system of social trust. As I argued above, competition, exposure to risk, and coercion create a few winners and lots of losers; the losers are rendered powerless, subject to forces outside their control and without access to social goods, legal protections, or organized resistance that might help them reverse their fortunes. This sense of powerlessness breeds contempt for moral norms because those who fail have less incentive to buy into a moral system that is stacked against them from the beginning, punishes their best efforts to be successful, and blames them when they don't succeed. Thus, the moral system built around promoting this ersatz form of self-reliance gives virtually everyone an incentive to defect from it. A moral system that gives everyone incentives to defect is not worthy of the name—yet this is what conservatives call the "values agenda." It is no mystery why one of every hundred American adults is incarcerated, an unusually high rate compared to that of other developed nations.[17]

This is the road to nihilism, and it is paved with conservative talking points about family values, freedom, and doing God's work. Conservatives have railed against the moral relativism and nihilism of Western culture, and it is precisely conservative hegemony that has brought them to fruition. Their war against evil has turned evil—it would be sublime if we didn't have to live it.

4

DELIVER US FROM EVIL

Conservatism's Big Idea—victory in the battle against evil—fails because the strategies and tactics conservatives employ undermine the social conditions in which morality can flourish. Nihilism, the belief that all values lack authority, is a real threat because the very conditions under which we acquire and maintain moral beliefs are fatally compromised by conservative policies.

However, the disaster that is contemporary conservatism is not simply a matter of strategies not quite being up to the task. In fact, the strategies misfire so badly that the goal of conservative thought consumes itself—the battle against evil exacerbates violence and mayhem. It risks becoming evil itself because conservatives misunderstand the nature of the evil against which they claim to do battle.

ORDINARY EVIL AND RADICAL EVIL

Conservative rhetoric about evil tends to be indiscriminate, but their rhetoric and policies suggest a distinction between two kinds of evil. When conservatives complain about homosexuality, abortion, and lazy welfare recipients who live off the public dime, they are accusing people who engage in these activities of lacking self-control. People who lack self-control cause great harm because they indulge their desires at the expense of other people. Of course, homosexuals, most women who have abortions, and most welfare recipients are not utter wantons. Lack of self-control is not the best explanation of their actions, though a lack of evidence never deters conservatives from making the accusation. Nevertheless, people who are excessively indulgent can become selfish and indifferent to the good of others, and when that indifference becomes habitual their characters turn vicious, though we would all benefit if conservatives limited their accusations to real criminals instead of people who are poor or different.

Evil caused by a lack of self-control is best understood as "ordinary evil"—Hannah Arendt famously referred to it as "banal."[1] It is ordinary because all of us are susceptible to it. Human beings are a battleground between desires that lead us to care for others and desires that lead us to obsessively focus on ourselves. It is neither inexplicable nor surprising that many people find it hard to strike the appropriate balance, especially when fear, anxiety, envy, anger, resentment, and social pressure stoke the self-obsession. Ordinary people in difficult circumstances to which they do not react well have caused great evil, but their motives are nevertheless ordinary.

The ordinariness of this kind of evil was displayed in the famous Stanford Prison Experiment conducted in 1971 by the psychologist Philip Zimbardo. Zimbardo divided student volunteers into guards and prisoners. The prisoners were taken to a replica of a jail where, over a number of days, they received increasingly humiliating and demeaning treatment from the guards. Despite the fact that these were ordinary people quite aware that they were participating in a simulation, the guards become genuinely brutal and the prisoners thoroughly dehumanized. For his part, Zimbardo played along and observed until his horrified wife, a social psychologist, persuaded him to stop the experiment because it was doing genuine damage to the psyches of the volunteer prisoners.

Zimbardo's interpretation of these events is that evil resides within the social system in which the evil occurs. None of the students were bad persons with a disposition toward violence or cruelty. Yet, given authority and the recognition that they were expected to act in an authoritarian manner, their actions quickly became vicious.[2] This sort of evil emerges especially in circumstances where individuals are subject to coercive authority and lack the independence or perspective to resist orders.

Conservatives argue that the profligate gain self-control and avoid evil when we force them to be self-sufficient and kneel to the authority of particular moral traditions. As I argued in the previous two chapters, this strategy is bound to fail because authoritarianism and self-sufficiency generate the very conditions that cause ordinary evil. Competition and coercive sanctions increase fear, anxiety, anger, and resentment while providing little incentive for being virtuous. More important, authoritarianism stokes the flames of ordinary evil. Self-indulgence is the special preserve of the powerful, especially when they have no check on their power. Authoritarianism sees to it that the cleverly self-indulgent occupy positions of unrestrained authority where they can do real harm to those subject to their will. As Zimbardo's experiments show, ordinary people often lack the ability to resist the dictates of nefarious authority figures. The worst villains in history, the Hitlers, Stalins, and Pol Pots, would have been pathetic losers, nursing their resentments in their own private hells. But they sat astride the powerful organs of state and ascended to their positions because the institutions they controlled bought into the conservative idea that there is a natural hierarchy, the upper echelons of which it is their right to occupy. And ordinary people were complicit because they lacked, as most of us do, the courage and judgment to resist. The greatest sources of ordinary evil are institutions governed by authoritarian leaders consumed by the energy of their obsession, and a frustrated, uncritical public all too willing to acquiesce. As I argued in chapter 2, belief in the absolute authority of a tradition entails submission to the authority of leaders who occupy positions of power within the institutions that support the tradition. Such institutions are the petri dishes that incubate evil, yet they are central to conservative moral philosophy.

Another sort of evil, which has increasingly come to dominate conservative rhetoric, is radical or absolute evil—hatred of the good because it's good. This is evil that is deliberately chosen as evil, a diabolical madness that we find difficult to understand because its very perversity makes it unintelligible. Radical evil has no connection to each conflict appears as an existential threat. There can be nothing more important than defeating it and no weapons ruled out of bounds for dealing with the threat. Any act, no matter how heinous, is viewed as simply the lesser of two evils. In comparison to the evil we try to stamp out, nothing we do looks immoral to contemporary conservatives. Hence, most conservatives were blithely unconcerned about the photos from Abu Ghraib, the routine use of torture, or the imprisonment of innocent people in Guantánamo. They do not see how such behavior is a stain on our moral reputation because, when compared to radical evil, it appears rather harmless.

This conflation of ordinary and radical evil is most evident in foreign policy. The conservative rhetoric of anticommunism, the exclusively military response to 9/11, the manufacturing of the case for war in Iraq, the rhetoric of existential threat posed by the nuclear ambitions of Iran and North Korea, and the demonization of minor potentates such as Saddam Hussein, Osama bin Laden, and Mahmoud Ahmadinejad all require the conflation of ordinary evil and radical evil. (Ronald Reagan, to his credit, rejected demonization when he negotiated with the Soviet Union.) In each of these cases, countries or leaders with modest means and serious but ordinary disagreements over resources, historical resentments, competing value systems, or geopolitical concerns are accused of being beyond the pale of rational discourse, incapable of acknowledging a moral appeal and responsive only to the threat of force. They allegedly pose an existential threat so dire that only massive military action will stave off our own extinction.

Domestically, echoes of demonization can be heard in the Religious Right's condemnation of homosexuality as a source of God's wrath, the rhetoric of opposition to abortion (which they often describe as a holocaust), the military response to the war on drugs, "lock 'em up and throw away the key" policies on crime, and even the electoral strategies of conservatives that characterize liberals as un-American. In the culture war, alternative lifestyles are mortal threats to America. The Bush administration's belligerence was not a product of Bush's arrogance or self-righteousness alone. It is the logical extension of conservative thought. Their utter dishonesty, stunningly stupid disinterest in diplomatic initiatives in foreign affairs, and stubborn intransigence on domestic matters express the conservative belief that opponents are incorrigible and the use of any means possible is always the only real option. Any attempt to constrain the battle against evil is seen as promoting evil.

The results of this conflation of ordinary evil and radical evil are serious and go to the heart of our current moral crisis. Because every conflict of interest is viewed as the product of an incorrigible intention, we commit ourselves to total, perpetual war and the constant manufacturing of enemies to feed the war machine, which creates more resentment, more grievances, and even more violent responses. Furthermore, we miss opportunities to resolve problems and conflicts because we fail to take opportunities to negotiate or recognize when we may share interests with enemies. By treating others as incorrigible we offer them no incentive to come to terms with their own behavior, thus defeating any possibility of getting them to change their minds. The methods and strategies required to defeat radical evil only exacerbate ordinary evil. To the extent we make this mistake, we become what we are trying to destroy.

THE LOGIC OF AMERICAN EXCEPTIONALISM

Conservatives find it easy to conflate radical and ordinary evil because of the uncritical belief in American Exceptionalism that tends to dominate our political discourse. As discussed in chapter 1, American Exceptionalism is the view that the United States is morally favored and thus has a special destiny to lead other nations. This inflated perception of our importance makes possible the following syllogism:

> Conservatives define evil as "hatred of the good."
> The United States and its policies are by stipulation good.
> Thus, anything that opposes our interests or our policies is evil.

George W. Bush's constant refrain "they hate us for our freedoms" flows easily from the reasoning contained in this syllogism.

It is hard to imagine a more dangerous idea because it means every conflict of interest between adversaries is a potential Armageddon. As a result, instead of winning the hearts and minds of people around the world after the 9/11 attacks, the United States' moral standing in the world is in tatters with large majorities in most human being requires also the nurturing soil of a society that takes the best side of our nature seriously. Self-indulgence and the lack of self-control can be overcome only if people have moral purpose; the self-assertion of the powerful is no moral purpose.

Conservatives seem to think that if you stamp out evil, the good will emerge. But, if what you have to do to stamp out evil is itself indifferent, callous, and vicious, the good will remain a fugitive. Conservatives love to quote gospel, but they must have skipped Romans 12:21: "Do not be overcome by evil, but overcome evil with good."

PART II

ROOTSTOCK LIBERALISM
A New Moral Vision

Conservatism's reign as a dominant political ideology has ravaged our moral stature in the world, compromised our ability to respond to new challenges, and has left our community and economy in disrepair. But if conservatism offers no foundation for American values, what is the alternative? Our current political landscape offers liberalism. Yet, despite liberalism's success in mitigating human suffering, and despite its historical place of honor as a term describing America's distinctive form of democracy, in contemporary politics, "liberal" has become a dirty word.

Although the conservative Bush administration has been widely acknowledged as an unmitigated disaster and Democrats now hold the Congress and the White House, conservative viewpoints are still widely respected in public discourse. As campaign speeches and attack ads have shown us in the recently concluded election cycle, conservative politicians, their words dripping with sarcasm, vilify any politician with a "liberal" voting record without further explanation, as if the mere belief in liberal ideas made a person as unfit for office as child molesters and rapists. Democratic politicians timidly ran away from the label, trying to assure voters that "I'm a conservative too," while real conservatives competed to demonstrate their reactionary bona fides. In the mainstream media, conservative commentators dominate, despite years of lockstep support for the failed policies of the Bush administration. More important, despite a wide consensus that change is needed, especially immediate economic stimulus to stave off economic collapse, there is little consensus about the shape of long-range political and social goals. Nostalgia for the liberalism of the past is unlikely to provide us with the conceptual resources to confront problems of the twenty-first century. Thus, despite a more favorable electoral climate for Democrats, there is still no alternative popular political philosophy that is poised to supplant conservatism. Moreover, the fact that conservatism was allowed to grow and prosper is itself evidence that liberalism needs revision.

Part 2 of this book aims to articulate an alternative liberal vision. Chapters 5 and 6 explain why the top-heavy, bureaucratic machinery of liberal governance fails to inspire voters and has lost its moral credentials. Subsequent chapters argue for a novel approach to refurbishing and articulating liberal values, which I call "rootstock liberalism." The meaning of this unfamiliar phrase will become clear only after the analysis that follows. It will be sufficient at this point to explain that a rootstock is the underground part of a root used for plant propagation. "Rootstock liberalism" refers to a cultural liberalism that develops the moral basis of society from the ground up, propagating relationships of social trust that provide the moral foundation of society.

5

HOW LIBERALISM
LOST ITS MOJO

The torrent of antiliberal rhetoric in mainstream political discourse is deeply paradoxical because much of what we admire about the achievements of the United States and its influence on the rest of the world has been a direct result of the triumph of liberalism. Twentieth-century Americans, under the banner of liberalism, initiated perhaps the greatest expansion of human rights and economic prosperity that humanity has yet witnessed. Franklin Roosevelt's New Deal, which included Social Security, unemployment insurance, banking reform, and consumer protections, helped provide economic security that enabled working people to sustain middle-class lifestyles. Massive infrastructure projects made electricity, water, and transportation available to millions of people. Mid-twentieth-century voters supported welfare that established a floor to help mitigate the effects of poverty, as well as greater access to healthcare and education for most citizens. Civil rights legislation enabled minority groups and women to share in this prosperity while enjoying legal protection from discrimination. Coalitions of nations formed international organizations such as the United Nations in order to encourage peaceful resolution of disputes and to extend human and civil rights to the underdeveloped world. Foreign aid programs, such as the Marshall Plan, helped devastated communities recover from war and famine. Millions of immigrants crossed our borders, extending the reach of American prosperity while enriching the cultural mix that defines the American character. Environmental protection became an established practice with broad-based support and was modestly successful at improving air and water quality.

Many actors made these achievements possible, but the common denominator that unites them is they involve government action that improves the lives of ordinary citizens. As a matter of historical fact, liberals tended to support these projects while conservatives opposed and tried to block them. Contemporary conservatives are still at work trying to undermine much of this progress.

This social and economic legislation expresses the following principles that define modern liberalism:

1. Each human being has equal worth,
2. Each human being is thus entitled to a degree of liberty that is compatible with the liberty of others, and
3. Part of the role of government is to guarantee equal treatment and liberty and enable individuals to advance their welfare.

The meaning and implications of the principle of equal worth and its relationship to liberty are complex. This is a preliminary account of liberalism, which will be deepened in subsequent chapters, so I will ignore much of that complexity for now. However, the meaning of equality is clear enough to be evident in the aforementioned policies that characterize twentieth-century liberalism. The moral justification for the use of government resources to provide a social safety net and social services to US citizens and to spread prosperity and freedom abroad is that the equality of human beings requires it. To fail to ensure equal worth would be to implicitly assert that some people are inherently less deserving than others because they are of the wrong race, gender, socioeconomic class, or nationality. Failure to acknowledge the equal worth of persons is a serious moral wrong. It shows a lack of respect for the qualities that make them persons and has led to a variety of egregious harms, from slavery to varieties of totalitarianisms. Thus, liberalism is a profoundly moral vision that takes the welfare of each person seriously and seeks to mitigate, through collective action, the cruelty and suffering that arise from humanity's darker impulses and the forces of nature.

Throughout the twentieth century, liberalism enjoyed considerable support despite powerful enemies. Although liberal principles are unevenly applied and continually under threat, throughout a significant part of the world, they have been successful at least to the extent that, compared to previous centuries, there is now less institutionalized injustice, greater opportunities for voting and education, better healthcare, and some acknowledgment of equal rights for women. But the idea of equal worth is a fragile idea, and its enemies are persistent. Human weakness and the burdens of life prevent us from acknowledging the value of some individuals, and people with an interest in preserving social and economic hierarchies often succeed in stamping out the idea of equality. It is not an idea that individuals through their own efforts can sustain, and both government and nongovernmental activism are needed to protect and advance the moral ideal of equality.

The liberal idea that each individual has value and is worthy of society's protection is Western civilization's most important contribution to the stock of moral beliefs that sustain human flourishing. Yet, as we begin the twenty-first century, liberalism is routinely caricatured as immoral and un-American. If attacks on liberalism were confined to conservative pundits and interest groups with a political ax to grind, we would have little reason for concern about the viability of liberal ideals. But the word "liberal" has become anathema to large segments of our population. According to recent surveys, only roughly 20 percent of Americans call themselves liberals, and Republicans at the end of the twentieth century rode to victory on the back of this wave of antiliberal sentiment that gradually but inexorably conquered much of the United States.[1]

Of course the social safety net, although under attack by right-wing ideologues, is largely still in place, civil rights and environmental legislation are entrenched in our political system, and we remain reasonably open to the rest of the world, despite the spike in discrimination against Muslims and other immigrants in recent years. Liberal ideas still govern us, but apparently we no longer think of ourselves as liberal. This is a dangerous development because, without the conscious awareness of how our prosperity and freedoms depend on liberal ideas, we are in danger of squandering liberalism's legacy. What explains the precipitous decline in liberalism's moral credentials? In this chapter and the next, I want to answer this question. This is not a question of merely historical interest, because, if the decline is to be reversed, we need an accurate account of why the moral status of liberalism has taken such a beating.

WHAT HAPPENED TO EQUALITY?

A variety of explanations have been offered for the rise of conservatism. As I argued in the introduction and chapter 1, the most plausible is that conservatism articulates a personal morality that many people believe responds to contemporary problems. Apparently, they believe liberalism is not so responsive. Many people think that liberalism diminishes in importance a wealth of commitments that provide fixed moral guidelines in times of uncertainty, such as self-reliance, religion, nationalism, and the family. Instead of taking these guidelines seriously, liberalism has offered an abstract principle of equality that not only fails to resonate with the personal concerns of most voters but also seems to threaten their place in the social and economic order.

In the name of equality, liberals have advanced the cause of minority groups that have, historically, been the victims of discrimination. Liberalism brought the moral and cultural issues of sexism, racism, and multicultural tolerance to the forefront of the political agenda and insisted that individuals fundamentally change the way they interact with others by treating them as equals. But now the white middle class must compete with these newcomers who threaten to take their jobs and supplant their cultural values with unfamiliar traditions. The idea of equality seems like a threat.

It was a highly educated, liberal elite that, along with the power of capitalism to satisfy any desire for a price, paved the way for the adoption of new technologies such as birth control that helped women advance toward sexual equality. But the sexual revolution and feminism challenged family norms and traditional ways of life that seem familiar and natural because they have been in place for centuries. The current controversy over gay marriage suggests to many voters that the drive toward increasing equality and emancipation has no limits, and we must as a matter of obligation overthrow all differences that result in hierarchies. Again, the idea of equality appears threatening.

Liberalism is associated with advocating the expansion of the welfare state with its bureaucratic excesses and high tax rates, which seem to reward irresponsibility and laziness. It is associated with a tendency to tolerate communism and criticize American foreign policy, activities that seem unpatriotic to some people. It is associated with policies to limit the public role of religion and has a tendency to promote activities that offend the moral sensibilities of some people, such as abortion, affirmative action, and same-sex marriage.

The economic and cultural waters are roiling and in the face of this turmoil, liberalism seems bent on undermining the sources of comfort that might lessen the turmoil—personal responsibility, religion, nationalism, and the family. The need for control over the circumstances of life in the face of a world seemingly out of control is at the bottom of the contemporary rejection of liberalism. Liberalism seems to not be answering this need, while conservatism promises a sense of personal control over one's life and circumstances; locates personal responsibility and moral obligation in a manageable, local context; and understands moral norms to be part of a natural hierarchy.

Thus, liberalism faces a daunting task in rebuilding its moral credibility because this context of personal morality and personal allegiances is the backdrop against which most people frame moral questions. Most people approach questions of morality by asking how answers to those questions will influence their lives and the people and activities about which they care. The more remote the object of moral attention from daily concern, the less compelling the moral claim will seem. Liberalism has always sought to extend moral concern beyond the manageable, local context, and this means the demands of liberalism will often seem abstract, with little relevance to one's personal life. Issues such as protecting the diversity of species, mitigating world hunger, or worrying about the effects of torture carried out by military intelligence on our world image do not have the immediacy of issues such as protecting your kids from porn or putting food on the table. Worries about the increasing inequalities of economic outcomes in society will not be salient for someone whose own prospects are improving through her own efforts. The deaths of countless Iraqi civilians are not as salient when our own security might be at risk from terrorists. A political perspective that argues you do not have to worry about these abstract, distant dangers has a natural advantage.

I am emphatically not suggesting that these criticisms of liberalism are correct or that they constitute a compelling indictment of the principle of equality. I argue in Part 1 of this book that conservatism is not an adequate response to contemporary anxieties. But I want to suggest there is a logic to the popularity of conservatism that liberalism must understand and confront if it is to flourish again.

Of course, there is a moral logic to liberal policies as well, but it is a moral logic that the American public over the past few decades has been unwilling to endorse. Poverty programs, the liberation of historically oppressed groups, peace and environmental activism, and a defense of secularism have their justification in the basic principles of equality and liberty that are at the heart of liberalism. They are largely consistent with the earlier policies of New Deal liberalism that enjoyed wide support. If the government is obligated to provide an economic safety net for the middle class, why not for the poor who need it even more? If an economic safety net is morally required, why not an environmental safety net for all of us? If we guarantee basic human rights for white men, why not for women and people of color? If marriage receives state sanction for heterosexuals, why not for gays and lesbians? If we value peace for ourselves, shouldn't we be reluctant to deny it to others? If all citizens are to have equal access to the institutions of government, shouldn't we be careful to limit the influence of any particular religion over the operations of government? But, unlike the policies of the New Deal, these more recent liberal causes, though grounded in a concern for equality, no longer enjoy a consensus. Why has the principle of equality, such a compelling idea in the heart of the twentieth century, been discredited at the beginning of the twenty-first?

I want to suggest that the early success of liberalism and the consensus that formed around these policies was not really about equality. It was about the self-interest of mainstream voters. Liberalism leaves a legacy of large-scale social programs that redistributed enough wealth to create and sustain a large middle class. It was in the self-interest of large majorities to support these policies, especially in the aftermath of the Great Depression, and it remains so today. In fact, recent Democratic victories are largely the result of increasing threats to the middle class as voters worry about their ability to maintain their standard of living in the face of economic recession. Despite threats by some Republicans to dismantle the programs, most voters still support Social Security, Medicare, unemployment insurance, and tax write-offs such as the mortgage deduction because they help to maintain their position in the middle class.[2] The process of moving large numbers of people into the middle class has been successful, especially for whites.

But as more groups of various minorities have made a claim to equal treatment and as this principle has been extended to social issues, commitment to this principle has fallen off because it no longer appeals to the self-interest of the majority. Welfare has been significantly cut; single-payer, universal health insurance cannot get a fair hearing; and support services for the poor are fragmented and unevenly supported. The moral tug of these programs was never large compared to the motive of self-interest. Once the majority of voters had been safely ensconced in the social and economic mainstream, there was little incentive to expand this mainstream to include those left behind. Moral commitment to the equality of persons seems to have only a limited appeal. This was especially true in the South since among those seeking admission to the mainstream of society were African-Americans. The exodus of Southern whites from the Democratic Party after the civil rights battles of the 1960s was precipitous.[3]

If self-interest is the most powerful principle explaining voting behavior, the arguments regarding inequality that liberals often prosecute have been notably unsuccessful. Economic statistics indicate that economic inequality has increased rapidly in our society. The top 1 percent of American earners have more than doubled their after tax income since 1990, while the income of the middle class has shown only very modest growth. This top 1 percent now controls more wealth than the bottom 95 percent. Real wages and benefits of blue-collar and low-level white-collar workers have shown little growth since the late 1970s.[4]

Democrats have occasionally raised inequality as a campaign theme, with little success. Al Gore, when his 2000 campaign for president was in trouble, adopted an economic populist theme. Although Gore won the popular vote by a narrow margin, economic populism was not sufficiently compelling to definitively defeat a candidate with a mixed record in business and governance such as President Bush, despite the economic successes of the Clinton administration of which Gore was an integral part. John Edwards, the vice presidential candidate in 2004, adopted economic populism as his main message in the 2008 presidential primaries, but the results revealed little enthusiasm for his charge that inequality is a moral failure.

When we think about what most people want out of life, the failure of inequality to capture the attention of a self-interested voting public in recent years is not so puzzling. Many people who lead comfortable middle-class lives are not interested in competing for a bigger piece of the pie. Of course, they would prefer more money to less, but their lives are not devoted to earning fortunes. They have consciously made decisions in life that will largely preclude earning a fortune, unless they strike it rich in the lottery. Instead of pursuing wealth, their lives are devoted to making sure their families are secure, their children are healthy and educated, and they have enough cash and leisure time to enjoy the simple pleasures of life. To accomplish this, they need gradual improvements in earnings or the products they buy to accommodate a modest expansion in their standard of living and to keep ahead of inflation, affordable housing and health-care, and credit cards to satisfy a more than occasional whim. Such a person wants an economy that maintains growth so she is confident of not falling behind and can look ahead to satisfying those desires that inevitably intrude—a new truck for Dad next year, new kitchen cabinets for Mom in two or three years, maybe a time-share on the lake ten years down the road when the kids are out of the house. From the standpoint of self-interest, such folks ought to be unconcerned about whether the high achievers and risk takers are taking an increasing larger piece of the pie. As long as the pie keeps growing and family income grows enough to stave off uncertainty, what happens to the rest of the pie is largely irrelevant.

Republican economic policies have produced this trade-off, successfully blunting any residual moral outrage that increasing inequality might produce. Their fiscal and monetary policies have promoted at best modest, incremental growth for the middle class while the high rollers abscond with fortunes. The fact that the confluence of business and government is fast producing a morally bankrupt kleptocracy does not enter the self-interested calculation.

Thus, the moral tug of equality in the abstract was never large compared to the motive of self-interest in advancing liberal causes, and today it exerts even less force. For many people today, liberalism has become a moral demand that imposes itself from outside their immediate concerns, an abstract and peculiar worry about equality that cannot compete with more palpable, personal concerns of earning a living, raising children, and protecting what one cherishes from a threatening outside world.

While liberal thinkers and activists were busy defining liberalism in terms of a principle of equality and trying to extend that principle to correct injustices, most Americans were thinking about morality as a form of life, a vision of how they should live, a set of concerns that guides them in making life's decisions. Conservatism has responded to that way of thinking. It has become an identity, a way of defining oneself that indicates a certain approach to life, a way of thinking about one's place in the world, and one's relationship to others.

For a variety of reasons related to fundamental features of liberal theory, and described in more detail in the next chapter, liberals are less inclined to think of their political views as a way of life and thus have not responded adequately to the need for a conceptual framework that can address issues concerning values. Thus, many people have increasingly come to see liberalism as, if not incompatible with their vision of how to live, at least irrelevant and unhelpful.

TOWARD A NEW LIBERALISM

The fact that mainstream America rejects liberal equality as a fundamental norm does not entail that liberal equality is indefensible or that conservatives are right to toss it in the dustbin of history. The goal of achieving a society that recognizes the equal worth of human beings is far from realized and it remains the worthiest of causes. But the foregoing analysis suggests some conclusions about how liberalism must go about rebuilding a progressive movement.

We have to acknowledge that we are indeed in a "culture war" and cannot avoid directly confronting the values issues that divide conservatives and liberals. Although perhaps effective during times of economic turmoil, continually shifting the debate to economic populism will not give liberalism a foothold over the long term on the fears and anxieties about cultural decline and foreign threats. The economic populist approach, though important as a component of liberal appeal, is too limited to sustain a movement that will reinvigorate liberalism because it implausibly assumes that if you satisfy people's economic interests they will no longer care enough about family, religion, or patriotism to rest their vote on them. Liberalism cannot succeed by offering such thin gruel. A coalition of the destitute will not be large enough to sustain a movement.

This does not mean we should abandon the economically destitute. We have a moral obligation to address poverty and economic security, but in the context of a broader, comprehensive vision of a good society and what it means to be a good person within that society. In other words, we need a moral vision that links equality (economic, social, and moral equality) to the everyday concerns of leading a flourishing human life, one that helps people think through the thicket of values questions that ensnare us. For too long, discussion of the virtues and about what it means to live a good life and to be a good person have been left to conservative "virtuecrats" such as William Bennett and Gertrude Himmelfarb, with their nostalgic, authoritarian platitudes. Liberals are deeply concerned about values, but we tend to understand all values under the banner of equality and fairness rather than articulating liberalism as a way of life, as providing answers to questions of how to live.

Of course, the Republicans have screwed up the economy so badly that mainstream Americans may dive back into the Democratic Party in droves to save their economic skins. Hence Obama's win, admit many Republicans, though glibly. But it should not merely be our charge to be a party of pooper-scoopers, cleaning up after an elephant parade. Rebuilding liberalism is not merely about winning an occasional election when conservative policies fail; it is about rebuilding the moral credibility of liberalism so that it can galvanize people to work persistently for a better society over the long haul.

Against my claim that liberals have abandoned cultural values to the conservatives, it might be argued that contemporary liberalism does address a variety of moral and cultural issues from abortion and family policy to privacy rights and national security. This is of course true but, as I will make clear in subsequent chapters, these policies are never articulated as part of a comprehensive vision of how social life should be constructed to meet contemporary challenges. The best evidence that we lack this vision is that we, until recently, kept losing elections, failed to increase the number of people who identify as liberal, and are continually being caricatured by the opposition as a collection of morally challenged interest groups beholden to the past, despite the fact that on most of the individual issues, *the public agrees with liberals*. If liberals have a message and a vision of culture, it is not making its way through the miasma of conservative cant that hovers over our political landscape like Los Angeles smog.

Given that liberalism must directly confront the values issues, the question is how to do so. Many commentators have suggested that liberals must learn to speak more clearly in the language of religion and manipulate more effectively the symbols of Americana and Southern culture.[5] As part of a comprehensive plan to attract voters, this suggestion is fine as far as it goes. The language of religion was an essential component of liberal struggles throughout the twentieth century, especially in the civil rights and antiwar movements. Given substantial levels of religious belief in the United States, any viable political movement must be attractive to religious folks.

However, as the foundation of a strategy for returning from political exile, this is a prescription for disaster. Though the United States is a deeply religious country, it is just as deeply pluralistic with countless religious perspectives flowering alongside varieties of nonbelief. Our secular political traditions are largely responsible for this diversity, allowing people to pursue their faith or lack of it relatively free of political pressures. The identification of religion and political power can only harm the religious imagination. Similarly, our ability to reach consensus on political issues is enhanced by maintaining some distance between religion and politics. The Republican Party's identification with the Religious Right has not been good for either religion or politics. Given the importance of secular political traditions and institutions in the maintenance of genuine democracy, since conservatives have elected to play the religion card, it is essential that liberals resist this trap. The defense of secular traditions has been a key element in liberalism—to sacrifice it for a few votes will destroy liberalism.

The advice to couch liberal values in the language of religion is sometimes a species of a larger argument that liberals ought to move further to the right on social issues, thereby capturing voters who may be attracted to liberal economic policies but dislike liberal positions on abortion, gun control, gay marriage, and foreign policy. In arguing that liberals must develop a comprehensive vision that directly engages the debates over values, I am not suggesting a move to the right on these issues. Liberalism's failure to recruit substantial majorities is not because it is wrong on the issues, but because its stance on the issues is seldom accompanied by a comprehensive, conceptual framework that operates at the personal level.

Liberalism has traditionally emphasized the degree to which individuals are dependent on the larger society for their welfare. We rightly perceive that outcomes are not always the result of individual choices and efforts but often reflect the impact of social forces that we should try, as much as possible, to bring under our control. Thus, the important moral issues have to do with human and civil rights, the provision of public goods, the alleviation of poverty, environmental protection, and the justification and conduct of war. We focus on moral relations between large-scale social actors that often require government coordination—public policy rather than personal morality. What we have failed to do is show how public policy is related to our moral identities, how a concern for public policy and social justice arises from the deeply held personal commitments, interests, and roles that make up the substance of everyday life in a liberal person's attempt to lead a flourishing life.

Conservatives are clinging to a world that is disappearing, a world in which old certainties and traditional values ruled; and they propose self-sufficiency as the means through which we can refurbish this imagined golden age. But self-sufficiency is an unrealizable ideal in our mobile, interconnected world, and the church, community, and family, by themselves, are not bulwarks against the abuses of the market or the permutations of culture. We live in a "values bubble" every bit as disconnected from reality as the Internet bubble of the 1990s or the housing and investment bubbles of the new century.

Money, information, populations, and culture are mobile, circulating the globe like an insistent jet stream invading every aspect of our lives while evading responsibility for the consequences. Yet, we are told by conservatives that if we are ill it is because we were not disciplined enough to prevent the illness. If we are unemployed, it is because we did not learn the right skills. If we are poor, we did not work hard enough. If tragedy befalls us, it is because we lack faith. The consequences rain on individuals and we must confront social problems and market forces with only strength of character as a shield. But the more we see ourselves as individuals, the less control we have over the conditions in which we live. In the so-called "ownership society" that conservatives promote, our freedom consists of the ability to choose between an infinite array of alternatives. But we have no capacity to shape the conditions under which our choices acquire their full moral significance. We embrace liberty all the more tightly as we watch it slip away.

It should be clear that conservative ideology represents no solution to this loss of agency. All conservatives can do is rant about values and taxes and leave everything as it is (or bomb foreign countries into bloody scraps in a desperate, naive, and self-deceptive attempt to export the very freedoms we are sacrificing). They offer little or no solution to the problems of global warming, financial crisis, poverty, or resource depletion, and their conclusions on destructive immigration patterns and terrorism are faulty. And as long as we see ourselves solely as individuals, we are powerless to gain control of these forces.

Liberalism can pick up the pieces of conservative irresponsibility only if it provides a vision of what counts as a flourishing human life that guides our political judgments. Today, liberalism seems like a collection of disparate interest groups—New Dealers, feminists, environmentalists, gay rights advocates, civil rights activists, and so on—with little holding them together except an agreement that the government is to promote the freedom and equality of all. So they come up with lots of policy prescriptions designed to curry favor with some group or other but propose no overarching vision of why people who don't fall into an interest group should support them. Too many people view liberalism as a kind of "anything goes" philosophy because it provides no guidelines for moral conduct aside from insisting on fairness. Fairness is important, but there is more to life than that. There is no way to

have been on the defensive for many years, moderating conservative excess rather than articulating a sharply drawn alternative to conservative hegemony.

Psychologist Drew Westen explains liberalism's recent troubles with people like Anthony. Using studies that demonstrate the brain's unconscious mechanisms for decision making, Westen argues that political messages do not help people form opinions but instead reinforce beliefs they already have. Their primary impact is emotional, not rational. Yet, Democrats and liberals typically base their campaigns on endless lists of policy options instead of giving voice to passionate narratives and strong messages that can motivate a distracted and apathetic electorate:

> Democrats, and particularly Democratic strategists, tend to be intellectual. They like to read and think. They thrive on policy debates, arguments, statistics, and getting the facts right. All that is well and good, but it can be self-destructive politically when alloyed with a belief in the *moral superiority* of the cerebral at heart, because moral condescension registers with voters. . . . They do so, I believe, because of an *irrational emotional commitment to rationality*—one that renders them, ironically, impervious to both scientific evidence on how the political mind and brain work and to an accurate diagnosis of why their campaigns repeatedly fail.[1]

Westen is right that Democratic campaigns are laden with sober, intellectual analyses that often lack the emotional power of the hate-filled screed and fearmongering that characterize conservative campaigns. In recent years, only Barack Obama with his inspirational message of hope and unity in the 2008 presidential campaign has escaped the wonkish recitation of legislative proposals.

There is a connection between this perceived lack of passionate commitment and an excessively intellectual approach to politics. However, it is not a commitment to rationality *simpliciter* that is the problem; it is a certain kind of reason, deeply embedded in liberal intellectual traditions, that puts some liberal politicians and activists out of touch with ordinary people and their circumstances.

This tendency toward intellectual abstractions became apparent many years ago under different political conditions with different actors. Although the demise of liberalism's political fortunes begins with Southerners bolting from the Democratic Party because of its support for civil rights legislation, the decline was exacerbated by complaints about arrogance and insensitivity. In the 1960s and 1970s, after deceiving voters into supporting the costly, unnecessary Vietnam War, liberals seemed largely indifferent and sometimes hostile to the returning soldiers, mostly working-class poor, who had sacrificed so much. Furthermore, liberals refused to moderate the tax burden on the middle class that paid for the war and Lyndon Johnson's Great Society programs that defined liberalism. Instead, they focused on the rights of minorities or environmentalism— worthy causes though not particularly germane to the lives of most ordinary people whose concerns were ignored. Liberalism seems to require detachment from ordinary concerns, an ability to dispassionately assess matters, which often appears as a lack of moral commitment. In this chapter, I want to explain why liberalism takes this cerebral approach to politics. But first we need to be clear about the basic commitments of modern liberalism.

WHAT IS LIBERALISM?

Liberalism is rooted in eighteenth- and nineteenth-century political thought that views the liberty of the individual as the basis of society. Modern liberalism, which emerged in the twentieth century, adds to this concern for individual liberty a powerful commitment to the equality of persons. Modern liberalism's commitment to liberty and equality is based on the idea that each of us, upon maturity, has the capacity to form a conception of how to live and to act on it. Although we are not equal in intelligence, physical strength, or other abilities, each of us is an independent person with the capacity to direct his or her own life. Tom Cruise may be more talented than Paris Hilton, but both are equal in their capacity to freely choose lifestyles of the rich and bizarre. Philosophers call this capacity to direct our own lives "autonomy," and liberals think this capacity for autonomy, when exercised rationally, is essential to our humanity. Liberal thinkers disagree about whether all human beings, in fact, care deeply about autonomy. Some people seem to enjoy their chains. But we agree that all human beings should have the opportunity to direct their own lives. The moral ideal of equality is the recognition that each of us has this capacity for autonomy and an equal right to exercise it.[2]

Liberty is essential because, if we are going to direct our own lives, we must be relatively free from excessive control by powerful external agents such as government. Thus, the history of liberalism is marked by the development of a system of individual rights that protects liberty and requires the government to treat each person with equal respect, which might come as a surprise if you have spent much time in a Senate hearing lately (or at the Department of Motor Vehicles), but this is philosophy—it's theoretical.

One reason why the capacity to direct our own lives is so important for liberalism is that liberals have been skeptical that there is a single best way for human beings to live. Human happiness is largely a subjective matter, according to most liberal traditions, and disagreements about what counts as a good human life cannot be settled by argument or rational reflection.[3] Thus, as long as we adhere to legal norms that represent our shared agreement to cooperate, we have to leave questions about how to live up to individuals—even people like Paris Hilton. (Sorry for mentioning her again; she's an easy target.)

Human desires being what they are, if individuals have sufficient freedom to make their own decisions, they will develop different conceptions of which goods to make a part of their lives. Thus, liberals also endorse pluralism—the view that many different ways of life ought to be allowed to flourish. Different strokes for different folks, as long as the strokes are not an ax splitting someone's head.

The problem is to get these diverse ways of living to cooperate. The traditional task of liberalism is to find a set of rules and procedures that all of us, regardless of our personal choices, can agree to follow. The legitimacy of decisions is based on the fairness of the process used to make decisions—not the substantive outcome of the decision.

The best way to discover and implement these rules and procedures is in a democracy that includes an extensive system of rights—property rights, voting rights, rights of free speech, assembly and due process, the right to worship as one chooses, and so on. Equally important for modern, egalitarian liberalism is the obligation to redistribute some income to ensure that all persons have the resources to direct their own lives. Unless a person has adequate shelter, food, healthcare, education, and an iPod, she cannot exercise her autonomy. Thus, the government, as the agent in a position to accomplish this redistribution, is involved to some degree in the economy.[4] When government policies redistribute wealth, however, the ideals of liberty and equality often conflict since providing the basic goods to those in need requires that we limit, through taxation, what others can do with their property. Thus, debates about striking the proper balance between liberty and equality are pervasive among liberals.

Beyond this commitment to rules and procedures that guarantee liberty and equality for each person, according to liberalism, the government must be neutral between various conceptions of how to live—it should not through its policies intentionally give an advantage to some at the expense of others.

THE RABID RIGHT

Is there anything in this doctrine of modern liberalism that would explain the accusation that liberals lack moral commitment and principled beliefs? Conservatives for years have been trumpeting the charge that liberalism's vacillation is evidence that it lacks a moral core or foundation. Their arguments routinely miss the mark, but before we can point out the genuine limitations of modern liberalism and construct a positive vision of a reformed liberalism, we have to remove the distractions of the right-wing noise machine that confuse the issue.

The conservative critique of liberalism is pernicious nonsense because it fails to acknowledge the moral significance of liberty, equality, and autonomy. The charge that liberals lack a moral foundation typically takes either of two forms. The first claims that liberalism lacks a moral agenda because it actively subverts religion by opposing school prayer and references to God in government institutions and public rituals, while endorsing policies that allegedly violate religious beliefs such as gay marriage and abortion. This criticism of liberalism assumes that religious belief is the only genuine source of moral value, and because liberalism is allegedly antireligious it must lack a moral foundation.

The obvious difficulty with the claim that liberalism is opposed to religion is that many liberals are devoutly religious. Eighty-seven percent of the American public claim that religion is important in their lives, so there are lots of religious folks voting for Democratic and liberal politicians.[5] Furthermore, many of the liberal causes that have contributed so much to liberal democracy have been nourished and advanced by religious folks and religious institutions, including the civil rights struggle, antipoverty coalitions, the antiwar movement, and the battle for immigrant rights.

Nevertheless, many liberals are secularists. Whether they are religious believers or not, there is deep concern among liberals that the relationship between religion and politics advocated by most religious conservatives, in which social policies must conform to particular, sectarian religious doctrines, is unhealthy. The reason for this concern is the belief that social peace, the ability to build consensus in a pluralistic society, and respect for the autonomy of individuals requires we preserve liberty of conscience on matters about which there is no settled agreement. Despite the psychological certainty of many believers, it is impossible to provide conclusive evidence for the existence and nature of God and the implications of God's word, an obvious point given the diversity of religious beliefs. To the extent that a claim is religious, liberals think that the state should not be in the business of assessing whether it is true or not, since no one knows how to assess its truth.

Many religious doctrines assert that only those who have accepted God's word and received the appropriate revelation should be treated as moral equals. But because the authority of God cannot be established through a widely shared process of justification, political decisions based on purely religious premises threaten to deprive individuals of a variety of citizenship rights. Because religious commitments enforced by government power impose sectarian beliefs on those who do not hold them, they deny the liberty of those persons and treat them unequally.

Although not opposed to religion, the liberal position does assume that moral claims are intelligible without being rooted in particular religious traditions and can be defended without specifically religious premises. This is a core element of liberalism—the belief that we can establish a basis for political cooperation without appeal to a religious point of view. Liberalism is not incompatible with religion. Rather, it asserts that in addition to religious values there must be nonreligious ways of understanding moral value. Only if that is the case can the process of forming a political consensus in a pluralistic society succeed and a variety of religious and nonreligious perspectives coexist. Thus, liberals are not hostile toward religion to the extent that policies advocated by religious folks are accessible to public reason. Liberals are rightly hostile toward religious points of view that hijack public reason by proposing claims accessible only to those who have received the "right" revelation.

What is the evidence that there are nonreligious ways of understanding morality? It is an obvious fact that nonreligious people as well as people who worship outside the Western monotheistic traditions are capable of acquiring moral character and living deeply moral lives, and they can provide thoughtful and compelling reasons for doing so. It is equally obvious that some devout believers are scoundrels. Religion is neither necessary nor sufficient for moral character. In fact, on most issues of moral importance, from norms forbidding murder to norms prescribing honesty, secular reason and religious revelation agree. This would be a puzzling coincidence if there were no basis for moral values outside of a particular religion.

As I argued in chapter 2, religious conservatives who insist that it is necessary for the public morality of Americans to rest on religious foundations must answer the question how, on that basis, we can organize a pluralistic society that preserves freedom of conscience, human and civil rights, and a basis for cooperation—I doubt they have an adequate answer. The separation of church and state is part of the genius of American democracy and the main reason why we have been reasonably successful at avoiding the sectarian violence that plagues much of the rest of the world. There is perhaps no idea more anti-American than the view that only a particular religion can provide the authority for public morality.

The second way in which liberals are accused of lacking a moral foundation is that liberalism is alleged to be a form of relativism.[6] The complaint seems to be that in striving to preserve the liberty and equality of persons, liberal tolerance for deviant forms of behavior has become so extreme that we no longer exercise any standards of judgment—anything goes. It is not clear why liberals are being charged with relativism rather than moral nihilism. Relativism is the view that standards of behavior are relative to a particular culture or social group and are therefore not universal. But, whether relativism leads to an "anything goes" attitude toward morality depends on whether the culture in question has restrictive norms or not. Moreover, there is no connection between how strongly one holds moral convictions and whether other people in other cultures also hold that conviction. The issue of relativism is irrelevant to what conservatives are worried about. There are liberals as well as conservatives who are relativists because they endorse extreme forms of ethnocentrism. But this is not a mainstream view and there is nothing about liberalism that entails relativism.

What about the charge of moral nihilism? Do liberals have an "anything goes" philosophy in which they are loath to make moral judgments about wrongdoing? As in much of the conservative diatribe against the Left, the charge is patently ridiculous. Liberalism's commitment to equality and liberty—and the qualities of respect, fairness, and tolerance that a liberal person must exhibit—are demanding moral requirements that require strength of character. It is not easy to be self-critical enough to work on our prejudices, to eliminate vestiges of racism and sexism from our attitudes, or to treat people we do not like with respect and fairness. It requires that we discipline many of our basest instincts in order to treat others with civility.

The moral task of goading society's institutions into conforming to standards of fairness and equality has been a long-term and demanding endeavor. It took liberal democracy many years to reshape our institutions to conform to civil rights legislation, a century of activism for women to gain access to positions in society, and constant vigilance to get society to take economic inequality seriously. Conservatives have resisted this demand for equality in part because it places too many demands on individuals and businesses, thus allegedly interfering with liberty. Conservatives cannot have it both ways. They cannot argue that liberalism places no moral demands on individuals and then claim that the moral demands are too stringent! To treat others as equals both in our personal lives and in the institutions of society is to take on a heavy responsibility, and history has shown that its implementation requires persistent moral focus.

The conservative critique of liberalism's moral failures is poorly conceived. If liberalism is deficient in its approach to moral values, neither relativism, nor nihilism, nor opposition to religion will explain why. Yet, liberal values have been unattractive in recent years; they seem to have lost their moral authority. It is important we discover the real reasons why.

LIBERALISM AND MORAL AUTHORITY

Modern liberalism's limitations are located not in its political ideals of equality and liberty, but in its conception of moral authority that provides a moral basis for these ideals and their defense in the public arena. Liberalism is devoted to instituting fair procedures that guarantee basic rights and wide access to resources in order to accommodate a wide variety of competing views on how to live. But herein lies the problem that all modern political ideologies face, elaborated by the sixteenth-century British philosopher Thomas Hobbes. How do we get fundamentally self-interested people, concerned most of all with their own freedom, to limit their desires enough to cooperate with each other and adhere to these fair procedures? Contemporary conservatives argue that individuals must learn to restrain their own desires through the influence of authoritarian social institutions— competition, fear of God, and the watchful eye of fathers, ministers, business leaders, police, and military forces keep us on the rails. (See chapter 1.) What is the liberal solution to the problem posed by Hobbes? The liberal answer is that we restrain our desires through our capacity for impartial, impersonal, unbiased reason. This answer is the source of modern liberalism's political difficulties.

Unlike Hobbes, who thought that we use reason primarily to figure out how to satisfy our desires, the liberal tradition has long argued, quite powerfully, that we can engage in genuine moral and political reasoning about what is fair and just. But the kind of reason that liberalism praises has a peculiar character that begins to explain liberalism's lack of passion and commitment. According to liberal intellectual traditions, our natural desires are fundamentally selfish, just as Hobbes argued. We can escape this selfishness and think clearly about our moral relationship with others, but only if we are not influenced by these selfish desires. Thus, moral reasoning must issue from an impartial point of view—that is the source of its moral authority. On moral and political questions, the liberal ideal is to be as impartial as a scientist in the laboratory or a judge deciding a legal matter. The liberal ideal of a person is someone who, when entering the public sphere to deliberate about political questions, leaves out of the deliberation her personal concerns, emotional commitments, cultural attachments, and the biases of her social or economic position in society. Only this impartiality guarantees that decisions by public institutions are fair to everyone and neutral between competing views on how to live.

From this impartial perspective, we can look beyond our personal needs and see ourselves as morally bound by a social contract in which we recognize our obligations to all human beings and special obligations to those with whom we are in political association. On this basis we can then decide on a set of norms and procedures for adjudicating conflict and regulating our common life. Controversial ideas about how to live that would not gain universal assent from this impartial point of view, such as particular religious views, should not shape public policy, and the government must not promote them because that would violate its neutrality.

Thus, according to modern liberalism, the procedural rules and norms produced by our impartial reason have moral authority. Liberal persons must be committed to regularly occupying this standpoint of impartiality—a standpoint that philosopher Thomas Nagel famously called "the view from nowhere"—which demands that we temporarily put aside the things we care about, the form of life to which we are deeply committed, the personal attachments and cultural references that give life meaning, and decide the shape of our public life.[7]

But this impartiality and neutrality is purchased at a cost, which explains liberalism's susceptibility to the charge of arrogance and complaints that it lacks passion and moral commitment. The deep problem with liberalism is that in striving for impartiality, we lose touch with genuine moral motives. By insisting that questions about happiness and the aims of human life are not matters of public concern—that we must be skeptical about trying to answer such questions—liberalism leaves us with a limited vocabulary for confronting questions about values. By adopting a conception of public reason that removes from consideration our personal attachments and private pursuits, liberalism leaves us with few motives for caring much about that public sphere that is vital to our success as a nation and our flourishing as individuals. This is why liberalism continues to struggle to capture the hearts and minds of voters, why it has ceded its moral credibility to the philosophy of conservatism that seems bereft of any moral content. Citizens seek a moral anchor, a way to conceptualize a good life, some place to turn in the face of economic and cultural turmoil—modern liberalism gives them only the thin gruel of impartial procedures.

LOSING MORAL WEIGHT ON THE LIBERAL DIET

The demand that our public life be governed by impartial and impersonal deliberation encourages an excessively bureaucratic approach to public policy that has helped fuel opposition to liberalism. Modern liberalism implements the ideals of justice and fairness by creating systems of rules that guarantee each person or interest group be treated uniformly. Uniform procedures contribute to impartial policies because they reduce the possibility that individual judgment and discretion might introduce bias and prejudice into our decision making.

The problem with this as a general governing strategy is that, within institutions, the rules and procedures become ends in themselves. Tweaking the rules, maintaining logical consistency, and managing systems so they comply with procedures become the focus of attention instead of satisfying the actual needs of persons to whom we are bound by ties of responsibility. The sense of personal responsibility atrophies, under such a conception of public reason, because it is easy to assume that personal responsibility is limited to a commitment to rules and procedures and that good intentions are therefore sufficient for moral outcomes. As a result we go through the motions of solving problems rather than really solving them, and the impetus for change and innovation is consumed with endless wrangling about process.

I will not dwell excessively on examples because most of us are familiar with the problem of insensitive bureaucracies. Our system of government regulations consists of endlessly detailed rules and enforcement mechanisms that are not only costly and intrusive but counterproductive when trying to solve problems. This produces the kinds of anecdotes that Philip K. Howard has made a career out of citing—daycare centers and homeless shelters that cannot be renovated, roads that cannot be built, teachers who are not allowed to teach, and a bidding process for government projects so slow and expensive that infrastructure is progressively depleted.[8] Government becomes increasingly incompetent because it lacks the flexibility to respond to human needs and appears more interested in adhering to its procedures than improving the lives of its citizens. Excessively bureaucratic government loses touch with the moral motives that, in a democracy, must drive its decisions. Yet, as long as the procedures are fair, modern egalitarian liberalism lacks the conceptual resources through which to mount a complaint.

The dominant image that a liberalism excessively devoted to procedure promotes is of the public official as unresponsive bureaucrat. Paradoxically, the demand for impartiality encourages another image of public servants as well—the self-serving opportunist. For at its worst, an excessive focus on procedure gives people the right to do wrong as long as the rules of the game are followed, as long as the action is legal or a majority has voted for it. Thus, Democrats and Republicans in Washington cut deals behind closed doors by compromising principles and doling out influence according to the power relationships set up by fundraisers, lobbyists, and their lawyers. This ruse, of course, is aided and abetted by the "village elders" in the Washington press corps who, through their refined, well-mannered, disinterested "opinions," manufacture consent for this thoroughly corrupt, though apparently legal, system.

The impartiality required by liberal demands for fairness and equality is impossible to achieve. Because desires and emotions are central components of our lives, human beings can never be genuinely impartial on matters about which we care deeply. Some people realize the futility of attempts to be impartial, but it gives them the cover they need to maintain the appearance of impartiality, to follow the letter of the law, and play by the rules, while always dealing themselves a trump card from the bottom of the deck. For others, perhaps less cynical, the ideal of impartiality means self-deceptively conflating their own interests with the common good, so they can enjoy a double scoop of self-esteem while they run the table. In either case, the moral sensitivity required for good governance is compromised. We have allowed the public sphere to be hijacked by those who are particularly skilled at wearing the mask of impartiality—the business leaders and politicians, "acting in the public interest," who always seem to arrange things so they come out on top. When the public inevitably becomes cynical about those in public life and vacates the public sphere, the Machiavellians reign. When liberal self-deception is added to conservative perfidy, it is no wonder we lack public institutions we can admire.

Even more troubling is the contribution of this pursuit of impartiality to the commodification of all aspects of modern life. Virtually every dimension of modern life can now be bought and sold and so must be sliced, diced, and counted so the profit can be measured. It is increasingly hard to distinguish work from play, news from entertainment, or art from commerce because everything must have measurable outcomes subject to the calculation of profit and loss. Calculation and self-promotion slip into every relationship as we increasingly value people for their performance rather than their intrinsic worth. Even family life is affected. Many parents view their children as little more than repositories of talents, strengths, and weaknesses that they deliberately shape by purchasing opportunities and experiences for them.

The pursuit of impartial reason is in part to blame. If procedures that distribute goods or opportunities are to be fair, we need a way of objectively and precisely measuring these goods. That means using a common yardstick to compare them, despite the fact that much of what we must compare is individual, unique, and particular. Thus, fungible, quantifiable assets such as money or measurable skill become the primary measure of value, despite the distortions that occur in assigning monetary value to nonmaterial goods. In transactions where money does not change hands or is not the sole determinant of value, some other allegedly "objective" measure such as test scores in education or clients processed per hour for public service agencies are employed as a stand-in, although these measures tell us little about the quality of work performed. Of course, these units of measure at any point can be easily converted into dollars and cents because the immeasurable has already been "quantified." Thus, satisfying the financial needs of various interest groups becomes the aim of every institution's activity.

For decades, politicians and analysts have argued that a variety of social goods should be understood as commodities to be bought and

Rather, as I will argue in the chapters that follow, regulations must be viewed in a wider moral context. Effective regulation that makes room for contextually sensitive judgment requires the motive and virtue of care—responsiveness to the legitimate demands actual human beings place on us that creates a culture of genuine responsibility and trust. When impartiality and efficiency are viewed as ends in themselves, they tend to expel from public life the nurturing activities of care, commitment, the bearing of burdens, the encouragement of growth and development, teaching, and healing. These activities do not flourish under excessively bureaucratic imperatives, because we cannot perform these activities while remaining impartial and dispassionate. While impartiality demands that we treat each person the same, care activities driven by compassion and empathy require that we attend to the specific needs of particular others. In summary, impartiality and excessive proceduralism foster the attitudes of the technocrat blithely carrying out her function without the sensitivity of human response. When liberalism succumbs to this way of thinking, it loses its grip on the genuine motivations of morality and has trouble making its case. Genuine moral authority resides in the demands that other persons make on us; the rationality of procedures is a poor substitute.

The problem is not that liberals lack compassion or empathy. The epithet "bleeding-heart liberal" did not arise unbidden. Liberal political initiatives are originally driven by compassion, but in the process of implementing and sustaining procedures that govern institutions, the "passion" in "compassion" often disappears. When liberal habits of conceptualizing solutions to problems shift the focus away from human beings and their needs toward rules and procedures, we lose the moral force of our proposals. And this shift seems natural and effortless because liberal thought sees its aim as managing competing interests rather than pursuing the moral good.

I am emphatically not rejecting equality as a fundamental value or calling into question the kind of practical impartiality associated with role responsibilities, which effective judges and arbitrators must exhibit. It is essential that our institutions are just and free of irrational biases, that we reason carefully and make sure our judgments conform to facts and sound science, and that we submit all ideas to critical examination. These are among the characteristics of liberalism that are responsible for much of the moral progress we have made in the past century, because they have mounted an attack against specific, pernicious, irrational biases such as racism, sexism, and homophobia. But our zeal to attack injustice must not lose its grip on the underlying motives of morality, which involve care, commitment, and compassionate response to the needs of others. Thus, impartiality cannot be the defining feature of a reformed liberal reason. Impartiality is a means to the end of justice but has no authority in itself. Cut off from the desires and passions of particular relationships and commitments to things we care about, impartiality will not fire the imagination, it will not inspire, and it will not feed the hungry or mount the battlements.

PRIVATE SELVES, PUBLIC CIPHERS

Modern liberalism demands of us that we take our role as citizens seriously and sustain a concern for public welfare. But modern liberalism is at war with itself because the ideal of impartial reason leaves citizens with few motives for entering and engaging the public sphere. The person most at home in a liberal society is capable of a divided self—capable of gaining some critical distance from her private, moral identity for public purposes while preventing that public face from encroaching too much on her private life. But this division in the self is difficult to negotiate and is unlikely to appeal to most people who prefer wholeheartedness to ironic detachment.[9]

The divided self is necessary because of liberalism's practical task. It must bring together vastly different ways of life that clash in a pluralistic society, and thus must endorse the overriding value of a broad and comprehensive basis for social cooperation. Political values like liberty and equality must outweigh other values. But this understanding of morality—as something designed for a public, political purpose—does not sit well with our nonpublic aims and attachments, which require a narrower but deeper model of social cooperation.

In public life, liberalism discourages the activities of care that characterize personal relationships by insisting on a wall of separation between public and private life. Yet it is through these activities of care that we form our moral personalities, acquire an identity, and discover meaning in our lives. Our patterns of everyday reason, and the skills we employ in making and implementing morally charged decisions are guided by the particular interactions we have with others with whom we have a relationship. We are guided in making moral decisions by practical concerns, situation-specific imperatives, emotional commitments, and the vagaries of individual, idiosyncratic moral personalities. Religion, cultural, and ethnic attachments and lifestyle choices shape this moral personality. However, the ideal of impartiality demands that this dimension of moral reasoning be curtailed when questions of public welfare or social cooperation are involved. Participation in political community compels individuals to suspend their most important commitments and attachments that may be basic to their identity and sense of moral integrity.

This is one source of our disagreements surrounding the relationship of church and state, controversies over political correctness, liberty of conscience, multiculturalism, immigration, and debates about who deserves what. What seems obvious to liberals from the standpoint of public policy does not seem obvious to people whose moral sensibilities are shaped by their personal relationships, and who do not or cannot shed those sensibilities when entering public life. It is not surprising that these initiatives are resisted, and that public welfare suffers. It is not obvious on what grounds we should condemn that resistance, for it is just these core commitments, which constitute a person's identity and integrity, that enable them to make moral judgments.

Morality is irreducibly personal and when we exclude that personal dimension, our moral capacities dissolve. As a consequence, many people view the public sphere as an arena of competing interests rather than a place of morally meaningful dialogue and interaction. Though liberalism aims at securing social cooperation, it introduces countervailing trends that weaken the basis of social cooperation as the public sphere atrophies.

As I will argue in the following chapters, care and our disposition to nurture and focus on particular individuals and their needs are essential to morality. When care is evacuated from public life because it does not mesh with the impartial criteria through which we evaluate the justice of institutions, public life becomes something to avoid or ignore. Modern liberalism is a gaunt, spectral outline of a moral point of view. Not only does it fail to say much about personal morality, its prescriptions often work against our personal moral commitments and styles of reasoning, thus ratcheting up the psychological costs of adhering to liberal views.

PRIVATIZING MORAL DISAGREEMENT

For modern liberalism, the strategy for dealing with such disagreements on moral issues has been to try to privatize morality—to remove controversial moral issues from the public agenda in favor of procedural rules that siphon off controversy and leave moral matters up to individuals. Religious preferences and doctrines, abortion, sexual orientation, the norms that govern families, lifestyle choices, attitudes toward social groups, consumer choices, and entertainment are among the issues that many liberals think should be private matters not up for public discussion. Liberalism imagines a big-tent society that is tolerant of and celebrates substantial differences between people.

However, this strategy, by its very nature, can have only limited success. This commitment to pluralism cannot be infinitely malleable or welcoming to all conceptions of how to live. The policies of government and other public entities cannot help but influence how we live. It is inevitable that a society constructed on liberal principles will require that some individuals seriously compromise their fundamental values and give up any hope of passing these values on to their children. Specifically, a liberal society will exclude ways of life that require excessive control over cultural products, coercive measures that severely restrict opportunities for people or that restrain individual expression. Individuals and groups who do not put such a high value on personal autonomy or on revising their values in light of cultural changes will not feel comfortable in a liberal society. Similarly, a liberal society that tries to impose norms of equality on private life will find many people resistant if their personal lives are characterized by relationships of authority. There is genuine tension between liberalism and traditional, authority-based ways of life, and neither side can privatize these issues because we live our lives as public and deeply interconnected individuals.

As a consequence, the boundary between what is public and what is

But to make this reflective judgment, what I care about must be something of genuine value. If what matters is not rich and deeply motivating enough to sustain my commitment over time, it will not sustain long-term judgments of satisfaction required for happiness. Happiness is more than a feeling because it requires a judgment about the quality and scope of one's activity over time. A life consists of all sorts of activities and concerns. What ties them together is the reflective attempt to see all of them as contributing to a judgment of satisfaction regarding the whole. In raising the question "Am I happy?" one is forced to look at life not as a series of discrete episodes, but as a whole that adds up to something of consequence. This comprehensive judgment ties the disparate parts of our lives together and encourages us to choose activities and commitments that promise satisfaction over the long haul, and more important, encourages us to deepen our care for that which is richer. For happiness we want gifts that keep on giving, because only such gifts will allow us to sustain the necessary judgment that one is happy. But of course I can misjudge the value of my activities, relationships, or possessions; happiness requires a judgment that must conform to a reality not wholly dependent on my will.

I call this conception of happiness "voluptuous care"—voluptuous because the enjoyment of the fullness and beauty of life is essential to happiness.[3] But such enjoyment is possible only when our caring responses to what has value enable us to successfully cope with our circumstances. Successful coping requires not just that we care *about* what is good; we must care *for* it, nurture it, make its integrity our own project, take up its cause, make its needs a matter of concern. This is especially true when the object of care is another person.[4] Our relationships with others for whom we care must be structured by regard for their intrinsic value. People neither function well nor respond positively when I regard them as mere instruments of my aims, and the relationship is likely to be nasty, brutish, and short unless we recognize the worth and vulnerability of what others care about.

This account of happiness is by its nature a bit abstract; a cinematic depiction will bring it down to earth. In order to sharpen our understanding of happiness as voluptuous care, I want to briefly describe a film in which such care is conspicuously absent, since we often best understand something by experiencing its absence. The film *Happiness* (dir. Todd Solondz, 1998) provides a particularly sharp though disturbing portrayal of lives overcome by delusions of happiness and lacking the crucial dimension of care. (Warning: For those who have not viewed this film, the "yuk" factor is high.)

If there is a general theme around which the film revolves, it is that self-absorption makes the search for human connection futile and ultimately destructive, leaving people with hollow, incoherent lives. But the film is also about how our judgments about happiness are often a façade. In this film, the warm, virtuous, prosperous surface of the American Dream dominates the story that the characters tell themselves about themselves. Yet, beneath the surface lie desires and fears that turn some of the characters into vicious monsters and prevent all from achieving happiness.

The film centers around three sisters, their families, and various acquaintances who filter in and out of the narrative. Joy, perpetually cheerful, sincere, but self-abasing and ingratiating to a fault, is hopelessly confused about what she wants to do with her life, though she insists "she's getting better every day, but Mr. Right has not appeared yet." Desperate for advice, direction, and support, her only confidants are her family members, who have always treated her with disdain and condescension. She hooks up with a thief, who after their perfunctory sexual encounter, steals her guitar and stereo, and then asks to borrow a thousand dollars from her, a request to which she reluctantly assents because—well, being a doormat is better than making no connection at all. Her problem is she wants too much to be liked—a kind of self-absorption—but cares little about the quality of that "liking."

Joy's sister Helen is a famous poet—beautiful though chilly and unkind—who incessantly brags about her boy toys and complains about the demands of celebrity, yet feels like a phony lacking the experience to be an insightful author. In order to give depth to her writing, she yearns to be raped but settles for arranging liaisons with an obscene phone caller. Her problem is that she sees herself only through her celebrity and views others only as reinforcement of that celebrity.

Finally, there is Trish, a pretty, cheerful, "happily" married housewife who never misses an opportunity to boast that she "has it all" tiful possibilities of planet Earth and its people, the American Dream is often a beacon of engagement and openness.

We are at our best when this engagement is complimented by the deep structure of care that sprouts from the seed of our personal attachments and extends its roots throughout the complex network of relationships that make up what is now a global society. Our ability to sustain our attachments to things of value depends on the quality of the people and institutions that we rely on in our profoundly inter-dependent world, and these people and institutions are not self-sustaining. We must care for them if we are to enjoy their value. The social systems on which we depend—governments, communities, markets, businesses, labor unions, schools, churches, aid organiza-tions, and so on—are not mechanized, self-correcting automata clacking away with inhuman efficiency while we savor their product. They are inhabited by people on whose capabilities we depend. The building of those capabilities—the maintenance of social capital—is crucial to the functioning of these systems.

In a world where the welfare of my family may depend on the quality of a healthcare professional's education in Detroit, public health monitoring in Beijing, farming practices in California's San Joaquin Valley, or the grudges of jihadis in Saudi Arabia, our ability to preserve attachments to things of value requires we extend our capacity to care outward beyond our immediate attachments to the relationships that make those immediate attachments possible. As a culture, we have often managed to extend our solicitude beyond the domain of the intimate and familiar, but we are inconsistent and prone to eruptions of myopic narcissism, as the recent debate on immigra-tion demonstrates. When we focus on our own interests alone, we are unlikely to notice the real needs of those on whom we depend, a myopia that gives rise to our war machine, our rapacious business practices that devastate communities, ineffective and wasteful foreign aid, and the scandal of homelessness and despair. The American Dream qualifies as a legitimate conception of happiness, but only when it acknowledges the deep structure of care on which any con-ception of happiness rests. The characters in the film *Happiness* are a personalized, domestic metaphor for the worst tendencies of the American Dream, when the desperate search for connection ignores the caring activities that are necessary to sustain those connections.

What prevents us from acknowledging this deep structure of happiness? Ironically, it is a derangement of liberty, the value that lies at the heart of the American Dream. It is a derangement that occurs in two steps.

LIBERTY AND AUTONOMY

Liberty is an iconic value that subsidizes the American Dream. Our restless, inventive search for value could not find expression without the liberty that allows each individual to find her own way. However, we have a maddening tendency to pervert this value that is so important to our way of life. The first step in this derangement is to conceive of liberty as a foundational value. "Liberty" means not being subject to the arbitrary will of someone else. This is usually interpreted as being free from excessive government interference—freedom from political tyranny. But why is liberty valuable?

Liberty is valuable because it allows individuals to direct their own lives, to make their own decisions, and express themselves through their actions. In other words, liberty is valuable because it enables autonomy. Autonomy is the foundational value at which liberty aims. It deeply matters to us that we are in control of our lives, that our prospects are not whipsawed by forces beyond our control or by ideas we do not respect. Thus, autonomy is a central component in any liberal conception of happiness that purports to make sense of the American Dream.[5]

There is empirical evidence for this link between autonomy and essential components of happiness. As David Marmot argues in his book *The Status Syndrome*, people who occupy progressively higher positions in a social hierarchy have progressively better health and greater longevity than the general population, even after controlling for social class and wealth.[6] Marmot argues that the best explanation for this disparity is that people in higher positions in a social hierarchy have greater autonomy. They have fewer bosses, less micromanaging of their everyday lives, and are less susceptible to social and economic forces that are beyond their control or understanding. Although Marmot's evidence focuses on the workplace, he clearly intends it to apply to social life in general. The quality of our interactions with others, especially regarding levels of coercion in those interactions, deeply affects our well-being.

That my actions should express most deeply who I am is a distinctive component of happiness understood as voluptuous care. Autonomy is essential to care because our motivations that underlie our propensity to care are highly individualized. When something in our lives demands a caring response, our motives to respond will be cut from the "crooked timber of humanity" (to borrow Immanuel Kant's famous phrase) rather than detached from a mold of standardized dimension. How we go about caring for something depends on the idiosyncrasies of individual personalities. Social institutions must permit this individualized response if they are to attract allegiance and commitment.

Liberty, because it creates the space for someone to lead a self-directed life, is essential for the development of autonomy, but liberty isn't sufficient for or identical to autonomy. A person can be free of meddling politicians and menacing gendarmes yet still not be in control of her life. What matters for autonomy is not only the absence of coercive actions by the state but the ability to use our freedom to accomplish something of value. Our ability to be autonomous depends on the physical, psychological, and material resources available to us. A person whose health is severely compromised or who lacks educational opportunities has diminished capacity for autonomy. If we can't think for ourselves because we are too easily influenced by authority figures or are unable to resist the coercive blandishments of advertisers, we will not be in control of our lives. If we are deeply conflicted about what we want, unable to evaluate competing desires, or if we lack the confidence to express our most important wants in our actions, no degree of liberty will enable self-direction. Thus, in addition to liberty, we need a full range of psychological capacities that enable us to assess desires in light of a conception of what we really want out of life and the self-control to implement that assessment, both of which require capabilities such as self-understanding and self-respect.[7]

However, when we pervert liberty and make it an end in itself, forgetting that the aim of liberty is to enable the development of autonomy, liberty becomes an impediment to the development of autonomy. Under the sway of this illusion, small sacrifices in liberty seem unjustified even when they might allow us to develop capabilities that are crucial for leading a self-directed life. This mistake afflicts individuals who, in the name of freedom, refuse to submit to a regime of education or skill building that will ultimately increase their abilities. It afflicts societies that, in the name of liberty, refuse to pay taxes to develop the social capital and infrastructure that will generate future development or to use affirmative action to enhance the prospects of victims of discrimination. When liberty is understood as foundational, the value of social goods, social justice, and community is never properly assessed; despite their contribution to our capabilities, they typically involve some constraints on liberty. When liberty is so misunderstood, the American Dream is compromised because we fail to assemble the resources needed for its realization. Libertarian approaches to government routinely make this mistake.

Furthermore, it is a very short step from seeking freedom from the arbitrary will of others to a situation in which we find our attachments and relationships weakened. Attachments to persons, activities, or institutions make demands on us that inherently limit our freedom. Thus, we often assume liberty requires detachment, insularity, or independence. This is the second step in the derangement of liberty, and it is deeply embedded in the American soul and political culture. This derangement of liberty can best be illustrated in the enduring myth of the frontier that continues to influence the American character long after the frontier has disappeared.

THE MYTH OF THE FRONTIER

The myth of the frontier continues to distort the American character because it assumes a conception of liberty that is utterly misplaced in contemporary life. The myth of the frontier is an extension of the idea of manifest destiny, a phrase referring to the mid-nineteenth-century belief that the United States was ordained by God to expand from the Atlantic to the Pacific. The frontier promoter and land speculator William Gilpin proclaimed:

> The American realizes that 'Progress is God.' The destiny of the American people is to subdue the continent—to rush over this vast field to

the Pacific Ocean . . . to change darkness into light and confirm the
destiny of the human race. . . . Divine task! Immortal mission![8]

According to this doctrine, America's identity was forged,
through the realization of God's dominion, by subduing the American frontier and the Native Americans who inhabited it. The need
for a "good conscience" required that these inhabitants be represented as ruthless savages whom the partisans of progress and civilization must destroy without compromise or scruple—violence was
a necessary part of the establishment of this identity.

In 1893, the historian Frederick Turner generated the myth of
the frontier by arguing that this historic destiny was made possible by
traits of the American character:

> To the frontier the American intellect owes its striking characteris-
> tics. That coarseness and strength combined with acuteness and
> inquisitiveness; that practical, inventive turn of mind, quick to find
> expedients; that masterful grasp of material things, lacking in the
> artistic but powerful to effect great ends; that restless, nervous
> energy; that dominant individualism, working for good and for evil,
> and withal that buoyancy and exuberance which comes with
> freedom—these are traits of the frontier, or traits called out else-
> where because of the existence of the frontier.[9]

This story of manifest destiny and the settling of the frontier
deeply shaped American culture by prescribing the character traits
that Americans ought to exhibit. As America began to feel its indus-
trial strength and burgeoning military might, the myth began to
creep into foreign affairs. President Theodore Roosevelt felt the pull
of this myth, with the United States' involvement in the Spanish-
American War and the affairs of the Philippines, when he claimed that
America must assert its virility by bringing civilization "to the red
wastes where the barbarian peoples of the world hold sway." With
Roosevelt, virility, violence, and civilization are deeply entwined.

Turner's 1893 essay had announced the closing of the frontier
since the territory of the United States was intact and geographical
expansion was seemingly at an end. However, the myth of a man with
his gun who is his own master dies hard. In a 1910 essay, "Pioneer
Ideals and the State University," Turner not only salvages the myth

but also advances its scope by arguing that the pioneer had just the character needed by the newly emerging industries of science and technology.[10] The captains of industry were the heirs of the pioneers of the Wild West. The self-made, independent man, who picks himself up by his bootstraps and makes a fortune using only his intelligence and strong will, is an icon of American capitalism and an extension of Turner's myth.

Although capitalism and culture have evolved since Turner's evocation of the myth, the myth's broad outlines are still in place. The idea that America has a unique destiny to rid the world of savages and bring freedom to the unwashed masses; the idea that being in touch with nature involves achieving dominion over it; the idea that an individual ought to be self-sufficient and that only the weak rely on government or social institutions to make their way; the idea that the essence of character is to take action, even violent action, in defense of simple, uncomplicated truths—these ideas are still with us, especially in the conservative moral philosophy described in chapters 1–4.

The myth is now embodied in countless Hollywood dramas, especially those starring the poster boy for the myth of the frontier, John Wayne. As Gary Wills describes Wayne, "His body spoke a highly specific language of 'manliness,' of self-reliant authority. It was a body impervious to outside force, expressing a mind narrow but focused, fixed on the task, impatient with complexity."[11] A tough, strong, courageous, and honorable man who stood up to evil and ultimately won the battle. At Wayne's death, President Jimmy Carter stated, "John Wayne was . . . a symbol of many of the most basic qualities that made America great. The ruggedness, the tough independence, the sense of personal conviction and courage—on and off the screen—reflected the best of our national character."[12]

But this praise of independence ignores one salient feature of Wayne's characters. Wayne often depicts a damaged personality so maimed by violence that he cannot himself become part of the community he saves. His need to be free of constraints was born not of a love of liberty—it was an acknowledgment of his personality disorder. Yet, the message that we take from these films, as well as others in the genre, is that civilization rests on the outlaw, the violent individual who cannot conform or assimilate, whose independence is absolute.

This legendary frontier has disappeared, yet the myth lives on as part of the baggage burdening our concepts of individualism, freedom, and autonomy. The myth of the frontier expresses the idea that freedom or autonomy requires self-sufficiency, entanglements with others always limit our freedom, legal and social norms are unreliable and a hindrance to progress, and acknowledging the needs of others is always an infringement on the basic right of individuals to be left alone. Echoes of various aspects of this myth were heard in President Bush's aggressive, go-it-alone foreign policy, his illegal surveillance and security measures, and his bizarre view that the president is above the law. More echoes reverberate in the absurd notion that every individual has a right to own a machine gun, the preference some Americans have for delivering their kids to soccer practice in a tank, in the "don't tread on me" attitudes toward taxes to secure even the most basic goods of social life, and in the widespread belief that social problems are simple matters of good versus evil, and their solutions a matter solely of having a sufficiently strong will.

The American frontier was a primitive society where the conventions of social life had little purchase. Life was boiled down to its essentials. Facing harsh and dangerous conditions, free of government constraints and unable to rely on social and legal institutions, only tough, independent, inventive, and self-reliant individuals could survive. This frontier has long since disappeared but the conception of an ideal person it spawned lives on. There still exist frontiers that we must conquer with courage and will—the frontiers of technology, sustainable living, and human understanding—but none of these frontiers require mute, damaged loners with small brains and big guns.

WE CAN DO BETTER

If our traditional interpretations of liberty and autonomy won't do, what are the alternatives? Traditional interpretations of autonomy place far too much emphasis on independence. Autonomy, the capacity to lead a self-directed life, requires the psychological capacity to resist excessive control by forces alien to the self. But the self is not an isolated module, sequestered from encroaching reality by the deadly, repellant gaze of the mind's eye. The self is cobbled together out of the persons and activities that we care about, and, unless we are utterly narcissistic, we care about external things—other people, human practices like baseball or religion, valued objects, but especially other people because nearly all of our activities have an essential social dimension. The unique, particular, individual self is largely a bundle of attachments, a history of relationships, and a set of capabilities through which we nurture those attachments. Without those attachments, there would be nothing to direct oneself toward and our freedom to choose one course of action over another would be utterly meaningless. Like happiness, the exercise of autonomy depends on sustaining caring responses to what matters to us, especially other human beings whose vulnerability commands our attention. Autonomy is inherently relational because the self is relational, constituted by those attachments that define who we are. Family relationships, enduring friendships, community, workplace relationships, and citizenship, to the extent they express what we most deeply value, are constitutive of the self and thus constitutive of autonomy.[13]

However, autonomy does not rest only on personal relationships. In order for our choices to adequately reflect the importance of these deep attachments, a network of crucial though less intimate relationships is necessary. These are the social systems, both public and private, on which we depend—the very same relationships that were implicated in the pursuit of happiness. It is a plain fact about modern society that our ability to express what we care about in our actions depends on a complex network of relationships that enables us to function. Given these facts, it is incoherent that I not care *about* this network. A liberal person is someone who cares *for it* as well, who takes some responsibility for the wider social context in which we live, because she recognizes her own ability to act depends on it.

When the derangement of liberty takes place and the relational dimensions of our being are forgotten, society becomes a collection of self-absorbed individuals reluctant to extend modes of care beyond the most narrowly drawn boundaries. We become a society in which shared interests and social solidarity are the exception, populated by individuals who imagine their freedom to pack a gun, guzzle gas, extort stock options, or purchase a politician is absolute, the consequences be damned.

The American Dream is a viable pursuit of happiness only if we avoid this derangement of liberty. Properly understood, liberty and the autonomy it enables are the ballast of the American Dream. But we need a new politics as well as a cultural consensus that does battle against the misunderstandings that corrupt our pursuit of that dream.

ROOTSTOCK LIBERALISM

This sketch of voluptuous care and relational autonomy outlines the basic moral commitments of what I call "rootstock liberalism."[14] Rootstock liberalism asserts that happiness and autonomy are rooted in our ability to sustain relationships of care, which must extend to the complex network of relationships on which we depend. A rootstock is the underground part of a root used for plant propagation. For my purposes, the term is a metaphor for the caring relationships—the rootstock—that generate and sustain culture.[15] Rootstock liberalism develops the moral basis of society from the ground up, propagating relationships of social trust that provide the moral foundation of society, a claim that I defend in the following chapters.

Rootstock liberalism is a liberal theory because it acknowledges the importance of autonomy as a central value and endorses a pluralistic society in which people are free to choose their way of life. Philosophically, it differs from modern liberalism in that it is founded on an account of human happiness that requires care for the network of concrete relationships on which we depend; and because it understands autonomy, not as the bare capacity to choose, but as a capacity for self-direction, which is dependent on relationships that enable self-direction and give it meaning. Though still pluralistic, this conception of happiness will be incompatible with forms of life that attempt to undermine the basic capabilities of persons or that make it difficult for people to sustain relationships of care that acknowledge our interdependence. In other words, it rules out the deceptive platitudes of conservatism.

Both autonomy and happiness thus have a moral component. The self is not a desire machine that signs on to morality only when forced by circumstance to submit to an authority, as both conservatism and modern liberalism would have it. Rather, it is a moral self through and through because it is constituted by relationships that can exist only through the disposition to care. Neither is the self a free agent operating independently of any attachments or commitments until she exercises her capacity to choose. The self is constituted by the capacity to sustain a commitment to what one cares about in our attempts to cope with our vulnerability. This, of course, involves choosing, but a choosing fraught with moral meaning that binds our ability to choose with our ability to nurture and provide care for something, to sustain our relationships and what is valuable in them. A sense of responsibility and commitment are not optional attitudes added on to facilitate social cohesion but are central elements of personhood and autonomy. Yet, the self is not identified by a particular kind of attachment—for instance, to a religion, nation, culture, community, or ethnicity—because rootstock liberalism acknowledges the diversity of attachments through which human beings achieve happiness, acquire autonomy, and cope with vulnerability.

I have been arguing that modern liberalism, by remaining neutral regarding what counts as a good life, leaves us with only very abstract political ideals as motives, introducing a split between public and private life that fails to provide a framework of cooperation that can solve social problems. Rootstock liberalism overcomes these limitations. Our common motive, in both public and private life, is the pursuit of happiness that requires as subsidiary motives the need to cope with vulnerability by sustaining relationships of care. Among the reasons I have for caring about seemingly abstract concepts such as social justice, equality, liberty, and the responsibilities of citizenship are the role these concepts play in enabling the relationships of care of a more personal nature. Rootstock liberalism is one way of elaborating Martin Luther King Jr.'s famous quotation from his "Letter from a Birmingham Jail": "Injustice anywhere is a threat to justice everywhere."

If personal happiness is so tightly bound to social justice, then liberal appeals to equality speak directly to us in our private lives, and public and private virtue have similar motives that mitigate the conflict between them in liberal society. Furthermore, we have reasons and motives that will secure the degree of social cooperation required to solve the problems of environmental stress, globalization, nuclear proliferation, and so on. If such a view can be implemented in political and social institutions, liberalism will have recovered its moral credentials from the usurpation that is contemporary conservatism.

Much more will have to be said about precisely how public reason is linked to private aspiration through the disposition to care. Nevertheless, working through conflicts between public and private life is not a matter of reasoning from a different standpoint—as an impartial spectator concerned only with doing what impartial reason dictates—but is a matter of weighing, in relationship with others, the variety of things one cares about and assessing their relative importance. Reasoning about public affairs does not require a new set of motivations, the magical suspension of self-interest, or high-minded altruism. It does require more sustained attention to how our own interests are affected by the welfare of others and why taking up their interests in dispositions to care can advance the welfare of everyone.

Because rootstock liberalism derives the moral motive of care from a substantive account of personal happiness and autonomy, it has a more robust political morality than modern liberalism. It frames moral issues in personal terms but explains why that personal point of view requires a public morality of commitment and care. The motive of care is not an optional attitude but is our most fundamental disposition toward the world.

This brief description of rootstock liberalism is quite abstract. I will say much more about what this looks like practically in terms of cultural and political institutions and political activity in chapters 9 and 10. But there is still something missing from my account thus far. The moral credentials of modern liberalism were strengthened by its commitment to cosmopolitanism and universalism—all human beings are moral agents and belong to the moral community. I have argued that we can no longer draw firm boundaries around our relationships of dependence and our dispositions to care must extend to an extensive network of relationships that transcend family and community. But this still leaves a patchwork of commitments limited by the fact that I am dependent on some people but not others. Relationships of dependence do not include all of humanity. Thus, the pursuit of happiness apparently does not give us reason to recognize the intrinsic value of each individual, only those who are part of the social networks on which I depend. By contrast, the cosmopolitan ideal extends far beyond relationships of dependence. Can our disposition to care extend to all human beings? The answer to this question requires that we understand the moral core that lies at the heart of every relationship, even the most fleeting and inconsequential. The following chapter will address these questions about the scope of the moral community.

8

YOU PUT THE LOAD
RIGHT ON ME

The moral relationship between persons is so central to our existence as social beings, yet so familiar, that it often escapes our notice, just as I imagine fish are oblivious to the water in which they swim. In these perilous times, we cannot afford such inattention. The revitalization of liberalism's moral credentials will depend on how well its institutions embody this moral relationship.

Artistic representations often provide the best access to phenomena so familiar that they hide in plain sight, crystallizing some profound dimension of human experience that goes unnoticed in the daily grind. Among the most profound is the penultimate scene in John Ford's *The Searchers*. Starring the American icon John Wayne as Ethan Edwards, *The Searchers* distills our moral relations down to a single molecule carrying the viral infection that keeps our fragile human hopes alive.

Ethan Edwards is a Confederate soldier recently returned to his homestead after the war. He is bitter, angry, and harbors a racist hatred for the Comanches who live nearby. Ethan's brother and his family have been eking out a living running the farm, but when Ethan leaves to chase rustled cattle, the Comanches burn the farm to the ground, kill the adults, and capture the two daughters. A search party finds only the dead body of his older niece, so Ethan and his partner, Martin, embark on a bloodthirsty, five-year quest to find the younger niece, Debbie. He discovers her living as a Comanche squaw with the brave who abducted her. Furious that she has assimilated to Comanche ways, contaminated and no longer of his tribe, Ethan tries to kill her and fails only because Martin intervenes and enables Debbie to escape.

Ethan, driven neither by love nor honor but instead by his racist obsession with sexual contamination, is now more determined than ever to dispose of this insult. He rounds up the old posse and attacks the Comanche camp, killing and scalping the Comanche leader and chasing down Debbie, who attempts to run away. Trapped in the mouth of a cave, Debbie cowers as Ethan bears down on her. As he gathers his will to murder, Debbie's terrified face brings him up short, rendering him incapable of carrying out the act that had driven his five-year quest for revenge and purity. He walks to her, picks her up in his arms, and says, "Let's go home, Debbie."

This scene depicts a plain moral truth—our moral capacities are provoked by the unmediated presence of a vulnerable human being. The cognitive boundaries we erect to keep out others, whether motivated by principles, doctrines, traditions, or fantasies of conquest and purification, can all seem small and threadbare when confronted by actual, living, breathing persons and their needs. Even the vicious racism of a war-addled, damaged personality like Ethan's, steeped in violence and heated by a five-year quest for revenge, is no match. The Lithuanian philosopher Emmanuel Levinas developed the metaphor "the face of the Other" to refer to this capacity of vulnerable people to cut through the tentacles of our will and intellect and set free our capacity for moral response.[1] Ethan recognizes in Debbie's "face" the fact that she has needs beyond his needs, a way of being that is not reducible to how he secs her. She does not belong to him and her vulnerabilities are not an extension of his. She is singular, with an identity all her own, and irreplaceable. Her vulnerability presses in on Ethan and holds him hostage—he cannot commit murder, even for a cause he believes is just.

This is the meaning of the metaphor "the face of the Other." Even a monster such as Ethan can have this epiphany, though among monsters he may be exceptional.

The "face of the Other" invades our self-satisfied conscience with the message that the singular identity of another person is of consummate worth. Human beings cannot be fully assimilated to the way we imagine them, and their vulnerabilities must not be exploited. Our response to the face is the paradigmatic moral response from which all other moral responses flow because this experience alone suspends our will and interrupts our drive to consume and exploit, enabling us to take heed of the needs of others.

Most of us have had this experience—a visceral response to the suffering or vulnerability of another person that induces us to act to his or her benefit. We feel this when the palpable presence of another person weighs on us, when the other person is not an abstract member of a category but an individual engaging oneself also as an individual. At these moments we are moved to sacrifice, to make the welfare of others the center of our concern.

The "face of the Other" does not refer literally to a particular face, and the "Other" is not someone who is odd, unfamiliar, or foreign. The "face of the Other" is a metaphor that picks out two fundamental dimensions of any person—her vulnerability and her relationship to her inner life, her interiorscape, which is beyond our comprehension. These are what we respond to in other people and they give human relationships texture and meaning.

It is our receptiveness to the command of the face of the Other that enables us to be moral beings. Without the intervention of the "face," our ambitions, fears, and enthusiasms trample any seedling of human difference left exposed to the elements. When we treat others as members of abstract categories, when we replace living, breathing persons with abstract ideas, legal rules, or principles of conduct, even if they are finely and acutely justified, they too easily become mere expressions of our will. We become agents of these intermediaries rather than advocates of charity and peace, and the face of the Other is veiled.

The face of the Other cannot be subordinate to the moral law, legal rules, the common good, religious doctrine, national solidarity or any of the other abstractions in the name of which we excuse violence. None of these imperatives quite capture the nature and significance of another person, and when we treat others as nothing but ciphers represented by these abstractions, we do them irreparable harm. Although it is natural to understand ourselves in part as Americans or Mexicans, Protestants or Muslims, these descriptions leave out what is essential about human beings—their radical particularity. As social beings, we must concern ourselves with the common good and specify the legal and moral rules that govern our common life as well. But through all of these practical allegiances and modes of self-understanding, the face of the Other must be allowed to speak, reminding us that a uniquely valuable, living presence is under constant threat from the categorical descriptions we carelessly use as placeholders for other persons.

We do not mobilize moral values by defiantly defending a principle or sticking slavishly to some phrase in an ancient text. We do not honor them by conforming to conventions or by setting oneself up as impartial judge and jury convinced of our rectitude and wisdom. We mobilize moral values by nurturing in ourselves the capacity to be held hostage by the vulnerability of others. When we act in the name of anything but the face of the Other, moral conscience is at risk.

Yet the political crosswinds of our age enjoin us to ignore the face. We are seduced by the dream of a system, by the idea that the operations of efficient economic markets, the laws of the state, the doctrines of a faith, or the regulations of bureaucracies provide us with all the moral guidance we need, enabling us to evade with a clear conscience the unsettling demands of the singular face that cannot be systematized. We are encouraged to draw platitudes from ancient texts, imbue them with false clarity and phony profundity, and call them traditional values, so we don't have to think or negotiate with the anxieties of the faces before us. We are implored to drink with mother's milk the cynical judgment that everyone is at bottom evil, making it an easy matter to erase the face through violence and mayhem. Our political ideologies would prefer that the face of the Other wear a veil so it can offer no resistance to the world of commerce and war. To the extent these ideologies succeed in obscuring the face of the Other, they lack a moral foundation.

AN ETHIC OF RESPONSIBILITY

In the previous chapter, I argued that the American Dream is dependent on relationships of care that extend beyond our self-interested needs. In this chapter, we see that these relationships are not wholly based on practical concerns or perceptions of similarity, familiarity, or solidarity. Instead, intimations of particularity and vulnerability, captured metaphorically as the face of the Other, provoke our conscience regardless of the categories to which we assign people or the ways in which we make use of them.

These relationships based on the provocation of the face are the foundation of social reality. Ethan's refusal to murder Debbie took place in a context of high drama fraught with devastating losses and dangerous passions. But this visceral response to the vulnerability of others is not a rare occurrence popping up only when brutes threaten lambs. It is a constant presence in our lives, the very foundation of the generosity that makes social life possible.

What could be more ordinary than walking through a crowded shopping mall full of strangers? Yet even in that cathedral of consumption, the face of the Other implicitly demands a modicum of generosity from me. Each person I encounter, numbly gazing at the spectacle of boundless commerce, commands me not to harm her. And I must respond to this command. In each encounter, it is wholly my responsibility to initiate gestures of good will toward the other person though I can know nothing of her intentions. My "welcome mat" must be visible but without the secure knowledge that others will reciprocate. Reciprocity depends on me making the first move. If I were to hold back, inhibit the subtle gestures of good will that emanate from me, wait for others to declare their intentions before proceeding past them, lurch between preparations for fight or flight until receiving assurances, mall security would descend on me like orcs defending Sauron's castle. Or to put the point more succinctly, any conversation that begins with "I might kill you" is going nowhere. The easy social commerce that our lives depend on requires that we obey the command issued by the face of the Other.

In each encounter, regardless of how inconsequential, the other person is commanding me to take a responsible attitude toward her vulnerabilities, beseeching me not to exploit them, imploring me to preserve her separate identity. She demands this of me regardless of how much I know or do not know about her. In every encounter, the other person designates me as someone who must be responsible, as someone who has the ability and obligation to respond to her needs—she commands my attention and care.[2]

As inherently social beings, we are implicitly aware of this command that others make whenever they are present to us in body or in language. But of course I am issuing a similar command to other persons as well. I command the other person to take a responsible attitude toward my vulnerabilities, to acknowledge my singularity. I depend on her forbearance, though my gesture of good will is not dependent on hers and hers not on mine, since each of us must make the first move.

These commands to be responsible and our willingness to respond are the glue that sustains society—fundamental facts of social reality to which we must attend. We could not function as social beings without them, because in the absence of these commands and the generosity of our reply, the only rational reaction to encountering another person would be fight or flight, which is rarely our response. Relationships, even between anonymous strangers, rest on trust and trust rests on the intelligibility of this command. Of course, what I should or should not do in response to the command issued by the face is dependent on context. Sometimes I should simply refrain from harming her. Sometimes I must actively promote her aims. Sometimes I must sacrifice my aims, as Ethan sacrificed his. But in any case, a refusal to exploit vulnerabilities is commanded.

Upon meeting a stranger, she makes demands on me—I am bound by her command to be responsible. Although I may refuse to acknowledge the constraint, it is already there prior to any communication or reflection. There is already moral authority in this relationship before anyone assumes a position of power. I am making the same demand on her and she is bound as well. But my command is not contingent on hers, and hers not contingent on mine. The command exists before any negotiation takes place; it is an implicit assumption, not the product of discourse, reason, or agreement. Neither is it a product of God's word or a characteristic of some tradition or particular community. Most important, it is not my choice. That I am being held responsible for others because they are dependent on me, and that others are held responsible by me because I am dependent on them, are brute facts of our social existence that originate in our fundamental attachment to the world as vulnerable beings and our sense of ourselves as agents able to act. This command to be responsible is the basis of social trust, a kind of ur-relationship that enables all of our other relationships. Without it, human existence as we know it would be impossible, and personal autonomy and happiness unachievable.

It is essential that any society seeking peace and human flourishing actively acknowledge, through its institutions and norms, our utter dependence on this responsibility to the face of the Other. Any account of the moral status of our social and political institutions must explain how responsibility toward the face is enabled and preserved. Yet, conservatism repels the face in an orgy of war and indifference, while modern liberalism is easily distracted from it by the wall of separation it erects between public space and private worlds and its focus on government procedures and the demands of bureaucratic organization. Rootstock liberalism, by contrast, is defined by its willingness to make responsibility toward the face the foundation of its politics.

A CYNIC'S LAMENT

It is a fact of social life that others hold us responsible for their safety; and it is a fact of human psychology that most of us sense their command and feel burdened by it. Only the monstrous are oblivious to remorse, guilt, and conscience. Nevertheless, the Other can refuse to act on my command and I can refuse to act on hers. Sometimes we do go to war. We often act irresponsibly and play fast and loose with social trust. Moral authority, unlike legal authority, is not backed by force. The face of the Other doesn't carry a gun—it issues a command with few enforcement provisions. Furthermore, the face of the Other competes with other powerful motives such as self-interest, affection, or a desire for solidarity with like-minded people. So there is ample room for the cynic, with his exorbitant hardheaded realism, to hurl invective at the face of the Other. Why should I acknowledge and respond to this command to be responsible if not forced into it, especially when others can so routinely violate it?

There are consequences to acting without regard for the face of the Other. The most immediate is that others will accuse me of irresponsibility. The other person always has the option to withhold assent to my treatment of her, to judge me as irresponsible. This capacity to judge me irresponsible is the only ethical power that the

Other has over me. But, of course, the only control I have over that judgment is assent to her command.

"Why should I care about this accusation?" asks the cynic. Why is her disapproval sufficient to encourage me to take responsibility for her safety? To answer this question we have to look at how the capacity for agency develops and how the absence of a moral concern for others disrupts our agency.

We develop our agency, our capacity to act, through our response to the face of the Other. As children we learn very early that our parents have minds of their own and vulnerabilities that our actions can allay or exploit. Through parental commands to be responsible, children learn to discriminate between desires they should act on and desires that are best left unsatisfied. The self develops as a structure of care motivated by the face of the Other—namely, her parents—in which the importance of encouraging trust is essential.

As the child develops, she learns that people other than her parents have vulnerabilities—expectations and needs that she can satisfy—and the structure of care develops as the child continues to mark a distinction between the desires that she happens to have at the moment that may or may not need satisfaction, and values that really matter, that must be acted on. In other words, the command issued by the face of the Other motivates the child to acquire and sustain self-control. As a result, by the time she attains full agency she will have already acquired a self that has internalized a desire to encourage and expect trust. At full adult agency, if all goes well, there is a reasonably coherent fit between desires, values, and her actions in the world. She achieves wholehearted integrity.

At least this is our ideal—to become a dynamic, uninterrupted will, a force of nature, with little confusion or misdirection, a self-satisfied conscience with a minimum of conflict between what we want, what we most deeply want, and our actions. Although impossible to realize in a complex world, this ideal of a dynamic, uninterrupted will is a hallucination worth having. The absence of internal conflict engorges the self with the joyful sensibility that life is under control. Our actions and everyday desires conform to what we value—actions flow from the self, not external forces. We are free and our powers seem unlimited. Anyone who has spent much time with teenagers recognizes the phenomenon.

However, although the face of the Other provokes the emergence of the self through the process of moral development just described, it also continually shatters the self-satisfied conscience. It renders inert this dynamic, uninterrupted will. Whenever the vulnerability of others is present, this coherence between what we care about, what we want, and what we do is being questioned, brought up short by the accusation that I must respond to the other's vulnerability. What I want or what I do cannot be reconciled with who I take myself to be and what the Other demands of me. The palpable presence of vulnerable others challenges me to be more responsible, trustworthy, and critical of my desires and actions. My freedom experiences itself as unjustified and must give an account of itself. This is the voice of conscience. Only by giving that account can freedom be restored. In interrupting the dynamism of an integrated self, the face of the Other challenges me to ask whether my actions and my desires live up to my core commitments. The face of the Other has such profound effects because it questions my commitment to social trust, which is the foundation of any relationship, and under normal circumstances is deeply woven into the structure of the self.

Only by responding to the command to be responsible can we repair this fissure in the self, thus restoring some measure of self-satisfaction and self-control, however compromised. The face of the Other is a constant provocation that demands the constant reweaving of the self, the refurbishing of the structure of care and my commitment to it. To turn away from the command of responsibility is to threaten the conditions of my own agency because my basis for action, the coherence between desires, values, and actions, cannot be assured. It is the ability to bear the weight of responsibility for others that confers whatever coherence the self attains. Without the provocation of the face, the self is disconnected from reality, wandering aimlessly from desire to desire, like bric-a-brac floating in a weightless environment. My taking up the command of the Other enables genuine freedom by anchoring the self in fields of gravity where choices have significance. In seeing myself as responsible, I enable my capacity to nurture that about which I care—it is the condition of autonomy as described in the previous chapter.

Yet, this is freedom rimmed with poignancy. Self-satisfaction is by necessity compromised and self-control only a matter of degree, for once the self is open to the face of the Other there are too many others to which we must respond. We cannot respond to one person's needs without taking bread from the mouth of another. We cannot be responsible without learning to live with the thought that ethics demands more of us than we can give. Moral strength is not found in the dynamism of an uninterrupted will, but in the integrity of a character that can respond to the face of the Other despite knowledge of the inadequacy of one's response. Strength of character lies in doing what we can while never forgetting our victims.

This visceral, immediate response to the vulnerability of others conditions agency in ways that loyalty to rational principles, ideals, or traditions cannot. Adherence to principles, ideals, or traditions involves only a monologue with oneself that imposes no burden from an unassailable Other that can accuse me of irresponsibility. Adherence to doctrines has no power to disrupt the will. It is self-satisfaction on the cheap, like playing Guitar Hero or whiffle ball.

Of course, moral risk—ignoring the face of the Other—does not make agency impossible. Some scoundrels manage to achieve something like happiness and their agency appears uninhibited. But the obstacles to happiness and full agency when incurring moral risk are substantial, the hidden costs are debilitating, the threat of nihilism ever present. The disposition to ignore the face of the Other inhibits my basic openness to the world, an openness that can be sustained only when vulnerabilities are mitigated through social trust. Freedom does not require anything like moral perfection. It requires that the provocation of the face be given its due and that one's response to the face is sufficient to sustain the social trust on which we all depend.

WHY CAN'T WE ALL JUST GET ALONG?

If being responsive to the face of the Other is so important to our agency, why do human beings routinely ignore the command to be responsible and allow the self to dissolve into incoherent fragments of desire? Although social life would be impossible if we always ignored the face of the Other, it is obvious that we often quite willfully treat others badly. Warfare, cruelty, and indifference are so embedded in human life that it seems perverse to insist that responding to the face of the Other is fundamental to the coherence of the self.

Part of the explanation for brutality and violence is that many children fail to develop as moral agents. Children who grow up in violent or chaotic environments or under excessively authoritarian parenting will be unlikely to develop the capacity to trust or be trusted. When children fail to acquire the recognition that persons other than their parents have a "face," trust will be limited to the family or to familiar others, thus inhibiting their capacity to develop comfortable relationships with others outside their immediate social context.

However, I doubt that our moral failures can all be explained by stunted moral development. Moral failure is built into the very structure of morality. Moral responsibility is a burden. Others impose demands on us that we cannot satisfy. Thus, we develop a variety of mechanisms to relieve the pressure of accepting responsibility for others. We engage in massive self-deception about the needs of others, construct elaborate fantasies of self-sufficiency, and attempt to isolate ourselves from the consequences of the disapproval of others—all attempts to maintain the fiction of a dynamic, uninterrupted will.

When these strategies fail we often accept incoherence as our condition. Because we always fail to do justice to the face of the Other, we must endure the continual disruption of our integrity—we never get our values to fully conform to our desires and our actions seldom conform fully to our desires or the shape of the world. The best we can do is to limit the damage so that the gradual erosion of a relationship we care about is avoided. Because some degree of incoherence is unavoidable given the complexity of life, it is easy to become comfortable with excessive incoherence, deciding that moral response is not worth the effort, and shunting the hunger of a conscience not satisfied to the basement of consciousness, where its moans are muffled by the garrulous cynic in the kitchen.

We can never eliminate all exploitation from human life. The command to be responsible is so demanding and disruptive that our social norms and institutions must act to lessen expectations by legitimating some forms of exploitation. For instance, in business transactions it is appropriate to exploit a rival firm's lack of financing when developing a new product. But it is not appropriate to exploit their weak security systems in order to steal their design plans. In baseball, it is expected that the pitcher will exploit a hitter's inability to hit a breaking ball, but it is not appropriate to doctor the ball or take his kid hostage until after the game. In every context, we narrowly circumscribe the kinds of exploitation permitted, and we must do so if the spirit of adventure is to flourish and our practices are to have the dynamism that enables growth. Boredom, torpor, and material deprivation are human vulnerabilities that morality by itself cannot alleviate. If we do not permit some forms of exploitation, the face of the Other is so excessively demanding that it is wholly disconnected from human flourishing. Yet these narrowly circumscribed eddies of permissible exploitation have a way of commingling with waves of hustle and enthusiasm. With excessive weakening of social trust, small, permissible exploitations easily become graft, greed, and grisly murder.

The illusion of a self-satisfied conscience is encouraged by authorities who preach doctrines of self-sufficiency that systematically obscure our dependence on others; it is encouraged by doctrines of national or cultural exceptionalism that construct much of the rest of the human race as evil or incompetent and worthy only of being manipulated or destroyed. When serious exploitation is encouraged as a norm, human vulnerabilities are viewed as opportunities for the fortunate to enhance their fortunes; we draw lines in the sand that carefully delineate the worthy from the noxious, and the face of the Other recedes. Without the persistent self-criticism invoked by the face of the Other, moral responsibility cannot gain a foothold. If this self-criticism is not encouraged by social institutions—if the confidence of the dynamic will is sealed off from the accusation of the face by institutions bent only on acquiring more and more power—social trust erodes and moral responsibility declines. The genius of liberal democracy is not that it allows us to choose, but that it allows us to choose the good. It enables the face of the Other to limit the power of individuals and institutions, thereby preserving our capacity for moral response.

Cynics have plenty of evidence that we are just trumped-up beasts with large brains, which we use for more efficient violence. Yet, despite our worst tendencies in this regard, an ethic of responsibility is our default condition as it must be for any civilization that has accomplished as much as ours.

THE EGALITARIAN'S LAMENT

Among the factors that inhibit the self-criticism provoked by the face of the Other are social conditions of extreme inequality. Wealth and power often insulate people from the consequences of their irresponsibility. They can generate illusions of invulnerability that deflect challenges to the self-satisfied conscience. When a person's social position makes it easy to avert her eyes from the needs of others, she can lose sight of the discrepancy between her values and her actions, and ignore the role that social trust plays in her flourishing. Reducing social and economic inequality is an important task, not because there is something inherently good about sharing a social class or income level, but because reducing inequality encourages the understanding that we share a condition of vulnerability that only cooperation can alleviate.

Yet, equality is a paradoxical notion. Although vast inequalities of wealth may encourage delusions of invulnerability among the wealthy, it is less than obvious that social and economic equality is a prize that we should seek. Without some accumulation of wealth and power, generosity is impossible since no one would have much to give. If wealth and power are too scarce, they become something to secret away and protect, and the provocation of the face will be obscured by anger and fear. A moral society must reduce the inequalities that inhibit our moral capacities, but not by aiming at an equal distribution of wealth that would reduce the surplus that enables our generosity.

In an important sense, human beings are not equals, despite our shared condition, because each of us is a singularity that cannot be compared, that resists being judged as a collection of properties that can be graded by a single standard. None of us are reducible to the accountant's ledger, the insurance company's actuarial tables, or the economist's demand curve. Though we have a common nature and shared interests, none of us relate to that nature in precisely the same way. My relation to my own experience is utterly unique. Any attempt to make our lives conform to strict equivalencies will be at best artificial and more likely tyrannical. We need a way to define the legitimate claims that people can make on society without the rules and procedures making a hash of everyone's life—without demanding that what is inherently unequal be made equal.

Social and economic equality are not achievable ideals because both our economic condition and our social relations influence and are influenced by the interiorscape—the inner life of persons—that is beyond comparison. The goods we acquire and the relationships we develop become part of our projects—a source of identity and community. They contribute to the distinctive, particular way I relate to my own experience, which cannot be compared to the way others relate to their experience. Our economic, political, and social relations must respect this unique particularity if society is to allow expression of the interiorscape. Even if deserved or justified, a radical redistribution of goods would disable this expression by wrenching people from their projects and inhibiting the pursuit of happiness. Even the wealthy and secure have a face and are vulnerable to loss. How, then, do we reduce inequality without trafficking in tyranny, without imposing measuring sticks and rules that homogenize what cannot be compared?

Part of the problem with our discourse on equality is that it is too often limited to economic, political, or social equality. In fact, it is moral equality that is more fundamental and makes our pursuit of the others intelligible. Society is a moral association only if each of us is able to issue and respond to the command of responsibility. Each of us must be able, from within the depths of our interiorscape, to speak sincerely, to testify on behalf of oneself; and each of us must be willing to mute our own voice when the face of the Other speaks. Moral equality requires that each "face" has a right to speak, to issue the command of responsibility. To permit inequalities in this regard is to deny a person the right to resist her death, alleviate her vulnerabilities, or give expression to her humanity. No society that aspires to decency can permit this. The idea of a liberal society is intelligible only if we assume that each of us are moral equals capable of generating the command of responsibility and responding to that command in others.

Moral equality is the condition from which social trust flows. Thus, we have practical reasons for wanting to ensure the moral competence of those around us. Social trust conditions all of our actions and can never be sufficiently fine-tuned to include only a narrow range of people. Daily commerce depends on the display of everyone's "welcome mat." Moral equality is not only a fundamental value in a liberal society but is part of the background conditions that any flourishing society must acknowledge.

Moral equality requires that we strive to reduce political, economic, and social inequality. If we are to be equally capable of issuing and responding to the command of responsibility, the procedural norms and civil rights that modern liberalism emphasizes must be in place. Rights to free speech and assembly, voting rights, habeas corpus, and norms that encourage more democracy are justified because they enable each of us to give and receive moral commands. Equal access to social institutions must also be guaranteed, for the "face" must be present in body or word if it is to issue moral commands; only if people can raise their voice in protest or affirmation can they accept responsibility for and command responsibility from others. The sense of moral self-worth necessary for people to accept responsibility for their actions and for the welfare of others can be achieved only through active participation.

This is why, for instance, opposition to gay marriage is such a travesty of justice. Gays and lesbians should have the opportunity to marry, not only because they ought to have the autonomy to decide such matters themselves, but because they have a right to participate in the sort of responsible concern and intimacy that characterizes the marriage relationship. Without the permission to marry, the ability to have a home—a refuge where unbounded, wholehearted, responsible concern can be given and received in relative isolation from the tragedies of worldly affairs—is severely compromised. The wholeheartedness to which relationships of intimacy aspire is compromised if society's agents condemn the relationship. As I discussed above, the integrity of the self is not immune to the judgments of others, which inevitably call the responsive person into question. When gays and lesbians are deprived of the right to marry, they have been arbitrarily designated by society's agents to be part of a group incapable of wholehearted, responsible concern; they have been, without reason, deprived of something fundamental to human experience. It is a pernicious, negative judgment on their moral capacities that is without basis—a form of bigotry. In the final analysis, persons are not kinds of things and there is no basis for social stratification based on arbitrary categories.

Moral equality has important implications for the distribution of economic goods, though it does not demand an equal distribution of wealth. The ability to make and act on moral commands requires a variety of capacities that are sustained by adequate shelter, food, healthcare, education, and so on. Because power differentials in society create strong incentives to ignore the face of the Other, a decent society requires a distribution of economic power that enables each person to be a full moral agent. The ability to make and receive moral commands depends on one's ability to cope with vulnerabilities and recognize the vulnerabilities of others—and this requires resources. In order to make and receive moral commands and to act on them, a person must have her physical and mental health, the capacity to form and sustain relationships, the autonomy to make decisions, sufficient wealth to sustain attitudes of generosity, and most important, the self-respect that comes from being able to express her interiorscape. The maintenance of social trust requires that each person gain enough social power to acquire a substantive voice in the management of her life. Thus, access to adequate shelter, meaningful work, education, healthcare, and environmental health are essential in enabling people to be moral agents. The destitute require access to those goods that are specifically directed toward satisfying basic needs and building their fundamental human capacities. This does not require anything like an equal distribution of wealth. Each person is due only those resources sufficient to satisfy fundamental needs and maintain the capabilities that enable her to lead a fully human life.[3]

There are countless ways in which one person is superior to another. We seek to reduce economic, social, and political inequalities not in order to eliminate social, economic, and political distinctions, but to achieve moral equality, to enable each person to develop, express, and act on the interiorscape that makes each of us the individual we are, and to develop the social trust that makes social life intelligible.

THE ETHICAL RELATION AND SOCIETY

The upshot of this Levinasian-inspired ethic of responsibility is that morality is fundamentally about the moral obligations that one person owes another. We are at our moral best when facing one other person or perhaps a small group of persons—when the relationship is direct and unmediated, when the singularity and vulnerability of the other can impress itself on me with its full significance. That moment when one's will is suspended, that fissure in the self, the visceral acknowledgment that the other person is vulnerable, beyond me, and higher than me is a necessary condition for an ethical relationship. This ethical relation of one person to another constitutes society. Society is built out of these relationships because, through the trust they generate, they enable our commerce and conversation.

Then we recover from this epiphany and ask, Who deserves what? and, What is fair? If our answers are to be just, they must be responsive to the face of the Other. The motive for social justice lies in our personal relationship with others. The problem is that these feelings of commitment weaken as they are dispersed over too many relationships and we suffer moral fatigue, not because we are weak but because there is too much to do. It is likely that evolution has designed us to be more responsive to familiar others because the conditions of life throughout much of human history demanded that we respond to local emergencies. But we no longer live the sort of life that can be consumed by tending our own garden. The challenge of contemporary life—liberalism's challenge—is to preserve our capacity to respond to the face when the Other's other and the other Other's other are present.

Modern liberalism has put forward the authority of an impartial, universal moral law accessible to reason and mandating freedom and equality as an answer to this challenge. But, although reason is important in giving us the big picture and determining how to carry out our obligations to others, it does not provide a sufficient motive for morality. It does not split the self asunder and demand its rebuilding. Reason's demand for impartiality crumbles when confronted with human desire. In the absence of criticism provoked by the face of the Other, reason will serve itself, swallowing the face of the Other in an orgy of vanity and hubris. It will assume that the Other is like me and that her needs are my needs. Reason will presume to know what cannot be known. Liberty and equality are thus left to fend for themselves—freestanding values that quickly lose their intelligibility as moral relations and degenerate into interest-group politics.

Conservative appeals to the authority of tradition are even less successful. When conservatives sanctify "our traditions," the face of the Other is painted over with a mural of mythological heroes and forced to wear the spangles of natives dancing for the tourists. For conservatism and modern liberalism, the ethical relation can exist only if mediated by some larger-than-life abstraction that, operating secretly behind the scenes, corrals our separated interiorscapes into a single encampment. The living, breathing person must be approached obliquely by a ruse. But traditions, texts, principles, and institutions do not have a face, only a mask that we mistake for a face. We cannot be obligated by these abstractions—only to the persons whose presence they mask.

By contrast, rootstock liberalism rests on the frank acknowledgment that nothing will save us but our own generosity. It views our ethical commitments in both private and public life as governed by a single motive—responsibility and care for the Other. Though the other person may be a friend, lover, fellow citizen, or stranger, with each relationship governed by distinctly different norms, each relationship is made possible by this ethical relation that underlies all sociality. All intact human relationships share the command of the Other as their foundation.

No institution, tradition, or principle can substitute for the generosity of the face-to-face encounter. Yet, we need institutions guided by principles and traditions to sustain social life. Most of our activities are supported by vast networks of unseen, anonymous actors—an ecology that requires sustenance if it is to survive. To see in this personal encounter, which I have been describing, the anonymous faces of those we never meet, we need institutions that enshrine the criticism of one person facing another, that nurture the fragile generosity and mutual responsibility that sustains social life. Only such institutions are worthy of being called moral.

As individuals, if we are not sociopaths, most of us, at least most of the time, recognize the moral claims of others, as individuals. Yet, despite an accurate analysis of our predicament, and despite our personal moral motives, we seem to have no secure route to collective solutions. Thirty years of conservative attacks on government and the intransigence of interest-group liberalism have eroded confidence in government solutions. Our political ideologies offer only blind alleys that promise more fear and isolation.

The first step in emerging from this bleak condition is to clarify a goal that cannot be subordinated to sectarian interests or co-opted by the avatars of corporate greed that today stalk the halls of our so-called public institutions. The most fundamental goal of our collective life is the rebuilding of social trust; for social trust is the anchor that makes whatever else we want an intelligible pursuit.

Rootstock liberalism is defined by its focus on leveraging our moral capacities in order to institute policies that build social trust, that encourage us to recognize and respond to the face of the Other—a liberal politics that does not shy away from calling itself a moral politics. The final two chapters focus on how we accomplish such a politics.

9

A CULTURE OF CARE

The force of morality, its motive, comes from the demands of palpable others who insist that I be responsible, who have the authority to make demands on me, and whose vulnerability and particularity motivate me to respond to their needs. The fact of being in a relationship itself constrains us, generates feelings of obligation and care, a force not unlike the force of gravity, weak yet persistent, easily overcome but constantly renewing its hold over us. These fields of force that insist we be responsive to the face of the Other form the basis of culture and give our lives content, meaning, and purpose.

Culture is dependent on these relationships of responsiveness and care because they engender social trust, which is the engine of culture. Without the belief that others are responsible and caring, our vulnerabilities overwhelm us, our sense of ourselves as capable persons evaporates, our ability to act is disrupted by doubt and fear. We typically think of culture as made up of institutions such as the law, religion, or the art world; or as patterns of linguistic behavior, shared traditions, or common beliefs. Culture is all of these. But underlying the institutions and patterns of behavior are a network of relationships of responsiveness and care that make the institutions and patterns of behavior possible.

We generate social trust through acts of generosity and care that we extend to others with no guarantee and often with no expectation they will be returned. A successful culture will find ways of making these acts of generosity and care more readily available, more likely to be welcomed and fruitful. Care, as I am using the term, is both a motive and a practice. To care for someone is to take the good of that person as a motive for my action for her sake.[1] The motive of care aims at benefiting someone or something directly, not as a by-product of or an instrument for some other goal, but because the welfare of that entity has become part of one's own system of value. But care also refers to a practice of sustaining that good, of performing the labor required to preserve what has value. Care is not about having warm feelings or good intentions. It is not fully expressed in merely caring about something. It demands more of us; it demands that we care for something; that we do the labor required to sustain connections and prime the wells of flourishing.

In a democracy, successful political ideologies must reflect the moral norms of the culture in which they are embedded. Morality inevitably shapes politics because through moral judgment we determine what is fair, cruel, or wasteful and who is worthy of respect, who is needy, and what matters most. But American culture does not consistently embody an ethic of care and responsibility *as a public philosophy*. Thus, for liberalism to succeed as a public philosophy, it must change culture from the ground up. "Rootstock liberalism" names both the foundation of trust and care that society must cultivate and a political consciousness that aims to build such a foundation.

Though the capacity for generosity is central to a viable political culture, this does not mean that society is possible only if we are suddenly overcome by purely altruistic motives. We are deeply self-interested and must be so if we are to survive and flourish. But self-interest is not our only motive. In fact, most of our actions are the product of complex, mixed motives, some selfish and some not, and the way we weave this generosity with our other motives determines our moral personality. We must acknowledge this generosity that is in our motivational mix and nurture it if the American Dream's promise of prosperity is to be realized.

An important part of our being generous and caring is to see ourselves that way, as part of our self-understanding. Yet, neither conservatism nor modern liberalism view generosity or care as fundamental to public life. Conservatism, as I argued earlier, is based on naked self-interest as our dominant motive and the power of traditional authoritarian institutions to control the consequences of that motive. This destroys social trust and with it any hope that we might live in a relatively peaceful, flourishing modern society. Modern liberalism assumes the same motive of self-interest but hopes that impartial reason might constrain that motive. It has produced majestic results but ran out of gas at the close of the twentieth century.

These impoverished intellectual resources have left behind a legacy of dysfunctional institutions and a failing culture. We have economic markets that create speculative bubbles, which shatter lives when they burst; an expensive, sub-par healthcare system in which nurses and doctors are overwhelmed and overbooked and patients feel powerless or threatened by loss of access; an educational system in which teachers are harassed and discouraged, students are apathetic, and the public disappointed; government institutions in which public "servants" are corrupt or demoralized; communities that are stymied by the cynicism of their citizens and many of them fraught with crime and violence; and a public discourse in which "spin" replaces sincerity. We are a culture that thoughtlessly trashes our environment, slips easily into useless and destructive wars, sanctions the torture of innocent people, and in the name of justice imprisons drug users in vast warehouses that incubate criminality. This moral blight is the product of the moral bankruptcy of conservatism and complicity on the part of some liberals. It is best described as a deficit of care, as a lack of genuine concern for the intrinsic value of persons and their cultures.

If care had been taken, liberal internationalists would not have been so quick to endorse Bush's war to occupy Iraq; if care had been taken, corporate liberals would not have looked the other way when cowboy capitalists took over the financial system or when the evidence for global warming began to accumulate. If care had been taken, liberals would not have acquiesced in turning prisons into warehouses for drug users in order to appear tough on crime. Their justifications would have seemed self-serving, lacking the proper motivation. It goes without saying that, if care had been taken, no conservative could have gotten close to power in this country.

Examples of corporate influence in science hit the headlines from time to time. We know of attempts to conceal the dangers of tobacco and asbestos, to deny the threat of climate change, and to cover up the lethality of drugs belatedly removed from the market because of inadequate testing procedures. Given conflicts of interest between the demands of science and the demand for profit, these are likely only the tip of the iceberg. The moral commitment of scientists to the activity of revealing the workings of nature for public benefit is weakened by excessive corporate control.

The most egregious example of corrupted professional relationships is the practice, which has become routine for conservatives, of filling positions in government agencies with ideologues or political operators who do not believe in the mission of the agency they are charged with managing. Conservative political ideology insists that government cannot work. Making it work would invalidate the heart of the ideology. Thus, conservatives, when they are in power, appoint all variety of incompetents and cronies to run important government agencies with the aim of corrupting their mission, while enriching themselves or the contractors they hire. Under the Bush administration, this practice became a form of art. The misadventures of FEMA (Federal Emergency Management Agency) in the aftermath of Hurricane Katrina are well known, but that only scratches the surface. Throughout government, career civil service staff were eliminated and replaced with unqualified managers who neglected the expertise of those who remained.[6] Neoconservative ideologues with bright ideas about cutting taxes and no idea how to build civil society were sent to Iraq to manage reconstruction. Recent college graduates with political science degrees were given authority to control what scientists could say and do in agencies such as NASA and the Environmental Protection Agency. In the Civil Rights Division of the Justice Department, prosecution of racial and gender discrimination nearly came to an end, as did the regulation of the food supply at the Food and Drug Administration.[7]

The idea of limiting the resources of government so it cannot function has been a stable element of conservative governance since the Reagan years.[8] Somehow, the American voting public bought the idea that managing the government is best left to people who care not a whit for the activities they are appointed to carry out. This is the most stunning example of how we are often oblivious to the importance of care as the proper moral motive.

At the core of any profession are standards of excellence that constitute performing that practice or activity well. These standards are regulated by the moral relationships that define the practice, which are relationships of care—teachers for their students, medical professionals for their patients, journalists and scientists for the truth, government officials for the public they serve. These relationships of care supply the motive for maintaining standards. For most professionals, the activity of meeting and advancing these standards is deeply meaningful, and society benefits because a profession's ability to perform its social function is enhanced.

By transforming them into profit centers for corporate interests, we eviscerate the professions by sabotaging the relationships and thus the practices and standards of excellence that define them. Of course, the professions need access to resources. Economic incentives are not always corrupting if they help supply these resources to supporting institutions. However, people who manage institutions must apply these incentives carefully if the integrity of the professions is to be preserved. If people who manage institutions, in demanding profit and efficiency, are insensitive to the moral relationships and standards of excellence that define a profession, the integrity of the practice is at risk.

In a society where everything is treated as a commodity and economic gain is the highest priority, only monetary value will readily survive and the goods realized by meeting professional standards of integrity and excellence will be battered by the incessant demand for profit or for measurement regimes that strive, inadequately, to precisely measure quality by measuring efficiency. The moral sensibility that sustains the practice collapses. Once again, trust is the victim. When the public harbors doubts that teachers, doctors, scientists, or other professionals are dedicated to maintaining the moral relationships and advancing the standards that make up their respective practices, the belief that society is a social system where ongoing social relationships can mitigate human vulnerabilities vanishes. Our society has not quite arrived at this doubtful denouement, but the public's discontent directed toward government and our systems of education, health, and media is not promising. Should we arrive here soon, the culprit will be the business model that treats persons and social goods like cans of soda. We are engaged in a dangerous social experiment that provides only external goods as incentives for acting well and fewer reasons to care for activities that should be deeply meaningful.

It is not only the professions that struggle to maintain the stability of moral relationships—a similar dynamic is loose in the larger economy. It was not too long ago that corporations were agents of stability in society. Employees typically would spend a lifetime in one corporation with steady career and salary advancement and guaranteed pensions. There were drawbacks to this model of corporate governance, but it provided employees with a sense of belonging and stable relationships that encouraged social trust.

In the name of freedom and efficiency, we have moved away from that model of stability to a new model of economy where mobility, flexibility, and risk are the norm. Capital is free to move where profits can be maximized, and that freedom has opened the globe to new opportunities for many, but new obstacles for others. I'll leave it to the economists to figure out if this has been good for our long-term economic health. But there are risks to morality because, once again, the relational dimension of autonomy is cast aside resulting in a loss of control over our lives.

As sociologist Richard Sennett argues, we have transformed ourselves from a society that values accomplishment, knowledge, and craft, all of which refer back to a history and set of stable relationships, to a society that places greater value on our capacity to change, to leave the past behind, to forget the old skills and acquire new ones in order to capitalize on new opportunities. Efficiency demands freedom and mobility and an atmosphere in which short-term relationships are the norm and strategic decisions must be governed by short-term thinking, cutting corners, the willingness to take risks, and the need to destabilize organizations to keep up with rapid change. Workers in this new economy are threatened by the repeated loss of meaning. Regardless of their efforts or skills, workers' jobs can be sent overseas or replaced by machines; high-pressure jobs in management or advertising can burn out workers before the age of thirty; and knowledgeable consultants can be instantaneously laid off because corporations must turn on a dime to fend off competitors. Sennett argues that employees are left with a sense of uselessness, wondering what their lives are all about.

In the face of this insecurity, our social safety net continues to be plundered—pension plans are underfunded or canceled, health insurance is in jeopardy, and proposals for cutbacks in Social Security are a constant refrain in Washington. Economic risk is shifting from government and business onto individuals and their families.[9]

As Sennett points out, most people cannot thrive in this environment. Only those who need no sense of having roots, who need no sustaining narrative but are energized by the sheer thrill of taking risks will feel fulfilled, as though the gunslingers of the Wild West have been reborn as investment bankers. The recent collapse in the housing and credit markets is the predictable consequence of the belief that a system built on risk and instability and oblivious to the need for social trust could be self-sustaining. The unwillingness of banks and other institutions to loan money and the reluctance of investors to invest, which precipitated the current economic crisis, is at bottom a deficit of trust, which reflects a deficit of care.

Under these conditions no one is sure who is friend or foe, loyalty is a liability, what counts as normative is constantly up for grabs, and fear and anxiety rule our psyches. Trust cannot grow in this environment because the conditions required for trust—stability and caring motives—are continually subverted. Meanwhile, the new economy is ramping up inequality, isolating the wealthy from reciprocal moral judgments while redistributing wealth upward, leaving the destitute even more destitute and with fewer reasons to buy into society and its norms.

These changes in professional and work experience have in common an utter disregard for the stability of essential moral relationships, some of which are intrinsically relationships of care, and others that require some level of care. Care is a disposition to sustain the value of someone or something, to take its flourishing as a motive for my action. Short-term thinking, mobility, risk, profit, and efficiency as dominant norms, and the faux independence from intrinsically moral relationships are disincentives to care, though they have become iconic markers of virtue for much of American society. Because the "new economy" is based on capital mobility and risk, it depends ultimately on financial markets rather than industry. Thus, the real power in the economy rests with people who lack the motives to produce beneficial outcomes from transactions. Financial leaders who are primarily concerned with moving money around to maximize profit care little about whether firms make good products, satisfy consumers, or benefit communities. Such an economy lacks the incentives to do what capitalism was allegedly designed to do—create value.

This deficit of care is the product of a moral regime, gradually unfolding over the centuries of modernity but accelerating rapidly in the past few decades, that emphasizes choice over quality and standards of efficiency above all other standards. It identifies what is rational with what is most efficient, takes our desires as given, and then asks how to most efficiently satisfy them. These two ideas—that choice is good independently of quality, and that what is rational is what is most efficient—are like wrecking balls smashing any moral value that gestates in the fecund climes of American life, because they subvert our motivations to care and inhibit our capacity to trust. As a consequence, our public life is increasingly characterized by apathy and cynicism and our private sector by instability, loss of meaning, and loss of moral commitment.

As I noted above, the recent collapse of housing and credit markets and the ensuing recession not only exacerbate instability and distrust; they also reflect and are caused by this deficit of care. Yet, we are not about to reverse all the changes that have shaped modern economies and go back to the old ways before the emergence of consumerism and globalization. The old way of life had problems as well: intractable, widespread poverty along with rigid moral identities that promoted insularity and bigotry. And the new way of life has many virtues—it is not only thrilling to reinvent the self, but life-affirming (if you can afford it), and our enormous productive capacity has lessened human suffering and will continue to do so if we make good decisions. Along many dimensions, our way of life has made substantial progress, and many economists who are sensitive to cultural factors and the importance of morality insist that we are better off with free trade, a globalized economy, and a mobile environment for capital.[10] The flexibility of our economy and culture is an asset in a global economy where productivity depends on making rapid changes to new technologies and new opportunities. There is no way to stuff globalization and consumerism back in the box. Yet, we must find ways of living well within the framework of a rapidly changing economic and cultural climate. Thus, it is essential that we rebuild the sense of social trust and commitment to moral value that has vanished in the marriage of economic man and independent man, a marriage sanctified by the rise of conservatism and enabled by the moral timidity of liberalism.

In order to renew American values, liberalism needs a countervailing self-image that opposes economic man and independent man—a self-image that takes relationships of care seriously, that views autonomy as a capacity made possible only by our connections to others, and that views our capacities to respond to the vulnerabilities of others, not as weaknesses to be suppressed, but as strengths to be nurtured and our most highly developed capacity. Such a self-image would have a profound effect on our outlook because it would pose different choices for us. We would come to see our lives governed not only by the rhythms of production and consumption but also by the needs of others who, often fleetingly and inessentially, come into our lives.

This is no utopian ideal—not some distant frontier or revolution that anticipates a new being. It simply asks of us that we consciously seek to maintain a persistent awareness of the moral authority of other persons, to find the motive of care as a fuller expression of who we are. We routinely acknowledge this authority within the circle of familiar relationships, but often fail to encourage those motives of care outside that circle. An ethic of care asks us to see those motives of care as admirable and to strive to make them more broadly applicable in our lives.

TRUSTING INSTITUTIONS

So how do we fix the motivational deficit of the public sector and the moral deficit of the market? The first step is to acknowledge our profound dependence on each other. Especially those who are powerful and priveleged must be aware of the ways in which their power and privelege is enabled by the poverty and acquiescence of others. But that recognition alone will not go far toward reforming institutions. Unless we support fundamental economic, political, and social change, charity toward the less fortunate will not solve problems but only make us feel good.

What would it mean for our institutions to be responsive to the face of the Other? It would mean that we think of morality as a process of negotiation through which we remain open to the vulnerability of those around us; that we adopt policies and ways of interacting that mitigate those vulnerabilities; and that we are attentive to the self-representations of others instead of imposing our view of them. It means recognizing that other persons have moral authority, not principles, traditions, habits, or hierarchies. Of course, institutions are not people—they do not have moral feelings or a consciousness that requires trust in order to function. But institutions are not utter abstractions either. They are made up of individuals who have the capacity to care, though it matters deeply that organizations support their caring individuals through its goals, strategies, and organizational system.

This openness to the vulnerability of others means that institutions must sustain opportunities for a shared process of deliberation and negotiation so that all voices are heard and the moral dimension of an institution's activity is a subject of ongoing discussion. Moral discussion must be an integral part of the functioning of an institution and a matter of public analysis rather than private conscience. In this way, we maintain a common moral focus despite the busy, compartmentalized structure of bureaucratic organizations.

Recognizing the moral authority of the other person also means connecting institutions to the larger communities of moral discourse in which they are being held accountable. Institutions and corporations are answerable to other institutions, their customers or clients, and the global community. Institutions form networks that essentially are relationships, which must be characterized by trustworthiness, attentiveness, and responsiveness.

Thus, the main conceptual revision is that we view organizations and institutions as webs of relationships regulated by the motive of care rather than merely a connected series of contracts regulated by principles of justice. The obligations of contracts do not exhaust the moral domain. In addition to contractual arrangements, there is a moral concern against which contractual arrangements must be weighed, the content of which is trustworthiness, attentiveness, and responsiveness toward the vulnerabilities of all stakeholders—an obligation to nurture and support both the people with whom we come into contact and the activities in which we engage. Effective governance must take into consideration not just relations between anonymous and homogeneous stakeholder groups, but in addition the highly contextual and particular relationships between actual individuals who belong to stakeholder groups. This is not to deny the importance of contracts. Care does not replace justice; it is an additional dimension, another set of factors that must be weighed in coming to a responsible decision about what to do.

The immediate objection to this proposal is that our institutions cannot function efficiently if we introduce requirements to care into relationships naturally characterized by conflict and competition. Care, according to this objection, is incompatible with the demands of efficiency and production. This is true up to a point. Efficiency may crowd out care, but only when we ignore our interdependence and the importance of the moral relationships that arise from that interdependence. Genuine efficiency and productivity—the sort that enhances human flourishing—depends on the quality of human interaction, which is enhanced by the motive of care. If the key ingredient in successfully executing agreements is the quality of the human relationships involved, then the virtue of care is necessary for any efficiently functioning organization or institution.[11]

But how do we acquire and sustain these capacities for care that enable the kinds of trusting relationships on which institutions depend? They cannot be sustained solely through a desire to enhance profit. Empathy and trustworthiness cannot be turned on when it benefits the organization and turned off when it doesn't. Agents who are routinely opportunistic give no one a reason to trust them and thus are incapable of sustaining the relationships needed for these necessary informal agreements. It should be obvious from the accounting scandals, financial misdeeds, and other fraudulent practices uncovered during the early years of this century that reputable firms with every reason to be honest in order to preserve future relationships and sustain confidence in markets nevertheless succumbed to the lure of quick profits, although the inefficiencies that resulted from these rapacious business practices were incalculable. It is simply no longer credible to argue that the motive of self-interest by itself will sustain relationships of trust and responsibility.

Purely self-interested behavior does not secure the trust required for contractual relationships, and relying on legal enforcement alone is expensive and inefficient. An atmosphere of empathy, attentiveness, and trust can exist only when stakeholders view others as worthwhile for their own sake—in other words, only when genuine care becomes a way of life. Think of the degree of cooperation between spouses in a well-functioning marriage. That level of functioning in an organization will obviously be efficient and productive—and it comes about because of the virtue of care. Paradoxically, genuine efficiency requires that we focus not only on efficiency but also on the quality of our relationships, so that we allow the intrinsic value of care to guide our actions.

The practice of Kaizen is one excellent example of how the virtue of care works, in practice, to enhance productivity and efficiency. Kaizen is a quality control strategy, often associated with the Toyota Production System, which is designed to eliminate wasteful activities and procedures in the workplace.[12] With the Kaizen strategy, all employees from the CEO to the folks in the mailroom, through cooperative effort, have the responsibility to continuously seek to improve their day-to-day activities, procedures, or the layout of their workspace, to make their work habits more productive, less tiring, and safer. Working in teams, with consultation and input from every level of the organization, employees devote part of their day to spotting defective tools that need repair, idle equipment, unnecessary tasks or unnecessary movement or energy used to perform tasks, systems that are not properly synchronized, examples of overproduction or underproduction, and so on. Employees learn to make changes, monitor results through application of the scientific method, and then adjust and adapt as circumstances demand.

The focus is on continuously making small improvements that, accumulating over time, add up to large gains in efficiency and productivity. But the aim of Kaizen is not just efficiency. It humanizes the workplace by creating a team atmosphere, eliminating excessively demanding tasks, improving safety, and especially through allowing all employees substantial input and personal autonomy by enabling them to continuously revise their work tasks.

I mention the strategy of Kaizen because it is a concrete example of how an ethic of care and responsibility builds efficiency without the dehumanizing effects of the command and control strategies we normally associate with efficiency. Through cooperative effort, employees gain a measure of control over their work lives. Although they are creating efficiencies that will ultimately lead to profit for their employer, employees are, at the same time, making their own lives better by systematically eliminating the nagging frustrations that make work a chore while enhancing their ability to analyze systems, evaluate evidence, and imagine and implement change. Most important, the practice of Kaizen requires building strong relationships within a work group—employees must learn to perceive the needs of others, sustain attention to those needs, and be motivated to help others. In short, Kaizen draws on the powerful motives that underlie our capacity to care jointly for others and ourselves. Kaizen is a workplace strategy, but the moral ideal that is operative in the practice of Kaizen is broadly applicable to a wide range of institutions and communities.

THE BIG PICTURE

Above I listed a variety of threats to our culture posed by the pervasive influence of models of economic efficiency. These threats included widespread instability in labor markets that weaken relationships, a sense of uselessness and lack of meaning that afflict those discarded by the economic system, high levels of mistrust that prevent the maintenance of financial relationships, the loss of a sense of integrity within the practices of professionals, and attitudes of powerlessness, cynicism, and apathy regarding public institutions, all of which undermine social trust, the crucial foundation of moral value. How does an ethic of care and responsibility help alleviate these threats?

The motive and virtue of care mitigates the effects of economic instability by institutionalizing norms that provide a stable basis for trust. An ethic of care does not view persons as cogs in an economic machine and does not define respect for persons solely in terms of their strength of will at overcoming obstacles in life. It recognizes the fragility of people and is thus willing to acknowledge that bad things sometimes happen to good people—failure in life is not necessarily a moral fault. Thus, a person's worth is not exhausted by her capacity to overcome any obstacle and is certainly not exhausted by her participation in the workplace or success in a career. In a society regulated by norms of care, a meaningful, useful life is one that participates in relationships of care, and this sense of meaning and usefulness is only partly dependent on one's successful participation in the economy. In a society that values caring capacities, loss of a job or loss of employment status need not lead to a sense of uselessness or meaninglessness.

Furthermore, a society that takes the vulnerability of persons seriously will accept responsibility for people who are victims of economic turmoil. The efficiencies or benefits earned as the result of imposing hardships on others (through layoffs, benefit cuts, etc.) are not the result of bad luck but are the products of conscious decisions to value wealth over persons, to place the value of economic efficiency above their welfare. Such a decision may be perfectly justifiable because wealth creation is a morally relevant value as well. But that does not absolve us of the responsibility to care for those who are disadvantaged. Those who benefit from economic adjustments are both causally and morally responsible for the outcome of those adjustments.

Thus, if an ethic of care were to become more influential in our culture, there would be a legitimate expectation, *offered without prejudice*, that the cost of economic adjustments would include compensation or some sort of substantial assistance for those who are too disadvantaged to adapt. Although we have in place programs such as unemployment insurance, welfare, retraining programs, and so on that alleviate some of the suffering caused by economic disruption, these are woefully underfunded, poorly administered, and limited in their capacity to alleviate the misery, sense of uselessness, and loss of meaning that comes from the loss of a job or sharp declines in income. These programs are inadequate because their beneficiaries are treated as losers in a fair competition rather than victims of conscious decisions, and thus the benefits are offered grudgingly, as if they are undeserved. Care offered grudgingly, with strings attached, and without a sense of generosity is suspect, because these are indicators that the motives are improper, offered to satisfy a mandate or guilty conscience rather than to help people cope with their vulnerabilities. As a result, our social safety net does little to encourage trusting attitudes on the part of recipients of aid.

Thus, an ethic of care is not only about what social programs we have in place or how many resources we devote to them—it is also about the motives and attitudes with which the care is offered. Government programs are effective only in a culture that supports their aims and shares the motive that gives rise to the program. That is why rootstock liberalism must be a cultural movement if the outcomes of policies are to have their desired effect.

Of course, by the same logic, people who are the beneficiaries of society's care are expected to contribute to society and assist in their own care as well. Trust is a product only of generosity that is not abused. Care imposes obligations on the recipients of care. But we can hardly expect the victims of our economic system to take responsibility for their actions if decision makers and other beneficiaries of the system don't take responsibility for theirs.

This generosity toward particular others, at least on the surface, does not seem to address the large-scale economic and structural problems, highlighted by Sennett, that a globalized market for goods and capital produces. The mobility of people and money means that most of our relationships will be short-term relationships that do not have time to develop into relationships of care or trust. However, a society regulated by norms of care will have two features that help to allay Sennett's concerns. First, in a society in which generosity is the norm there is less mistrust to overcome. Thus, it is easier for short-term relationships to be genuine caring relationships. Second, in such a society, we would actively seek out more stable relationships by not adopting norms of efficiency as the default condition. In a society like ours constructed around norms of efficiency, it is often simply taken for granted that reason requires that we undergo any change that promises more opportunity, more choices, or greater profit. But in a society regulated by care, though we will not ignore matters of opportunity, choice, or profit, these will not be overriding. They will not constitute the rational default position.

In a society in which the norms of care regulate a variety of our activities and the motive of care plays a more dominant role in our conception of moral character, it goes without saying that social trust will grow as well. We will have a higher level of legitimate confidence in the intentions of others and more reason to assume they are well intentioned. Social trust is an effective foil for cynicism and apathy.

Furthermore, a culture of care will stop the dangerous erosion of the integrity of professional practices. Because it insists that we "get the relationships right" and sustain motives of care, a culture of care will regulate external influences on the professions that distort relationships and thus distort incentives. A culture of care resists the dehumanization of the professions and resists the processes that turn humans into commodities, though it does not ignore the benefits that productivity and efficiency gains bring about. A culture of care seeks to discover and preserve the human-relational dimension of life in the midst of technological advance, a form of creative opposition that does not merely oppose but opposes with the intent to preserve what is good about innovation. It resists the inappropriate imperialism of the profit motive as well as the ennui of corporate or bureaucratic careerism, without sacrificing the goods of modernity.

Most important, a culture of care will reorder our value judgments and priorities. Instead of viewing corporate power and military strength as the most morally admirable pursuits, we will come to see the tasks of preserving our environment, raising and educating children, and achieving peace as deserving more praise and resources.

A culture of care promotes the health of the relationships of its members. The pursuit of self-interest and the assertion of individual rights takes place within these relationships that make them possible. No family or friendship could survive for long if the participants cared only for themselves and ignored the needs of others. The same holds true of a society or culture. Without relationships of care we cannot have a functioning legal, economic, or political system. Rootstock liberalism cultivates this culture of care by building communities that sustain the integrity of cooperative activities.

This chapter has not focused on particular government policies or programs—the standard fare of liberal, political discourse. It has been about attitudes, qualities of character, and motives—specifically the motive of care. This is important because policies and programs are realized within a culture of concrete relationships that must be of a certain quality if the policies and programs are to be effective. This is the cultural dimension that liberalism has for too long ignored. However, such a culture cannot be built in a political vacuum. In the next chapter I focus on the policies that will help us realize such a culture.

10

CHANGING THE
MORAL PARADIGM

I have been arguing that sustained, progressive political change will require cultural change. But how do we build such a culture? Its foundation is our willingness to acknowledge the face of the Other, reinforced by the recognition that our capacity to care in both private and public life is the most admirable part of who we are. But these recognitions are individual acts with public, political ends. What do the politics look like, and what incentives will encourage the caring side of our nature to be more prominent?

Twentieth-century liberalism endorsed the central role of government in creating infrastructure; maintaining free, fair, competitive markets; investing in human capabilities; and protecting people from market failure. But critics accused this brand of liberalism of throwing money at problems, of trying to micromanage peoples' lives, and of creating large, cumbersome, expensive bureaucracies to carry out government functions that were insensitive to the needs of the people they were trying to help. A twenty-first-century progressive liberalism, if it is to maintain power, must avoid these pitfalls.

Rootstock liberalism endorses the essential role of government but views that role from the perspective of the health of relationships, not system imperatives. The role of government is to facilitate relations of care, not to tell everyone what to do. It encourages cooperation, empathy, and sensitivity toward the vulnerabilities of people affected by a policy, eliminates obstacles to their expression, and encourages individuals to formulate their own solutions. Rootstock liberalism is devoted to sustaining conditions in which social trust can flourish without reliance on authoritarian measures that subvert trust. It leaves people and their communities free to imagine alternatives and implement creative solutions to their problems.

THE DOMESTIC CARE AGENDA

The essential policies promote relationships of care as a moral ideal rather than the competitive economic relationships that we now hold in such esteem. This means enhancing the salary and prestige of care workers, especially those who care for children but also those who care for the elderly and the disabled. When children grow up to be productive members of society, and dependent people are cared for, all of us benefit. In fact, business and government receive an enormous subsidy through unpaid care work. The social norms that create productive workers, cooperative citizens, and well-cared-for senior citizens are reproduced from generation to generation through the efforts of care workers. But the parents who care for children or the family members who aid dependent people are not compensated. Thus, the rest of us are free riders—we receive a benefit we have not paid for. The strongest indicator that we suffer from a care deficit is the fact that, in a society that uses wealth and income as a measure of success, much care work comes with little or no compensation.[1]

No doubt it is difficult to know how to compensate some care workers. Because care work is largely nonmarket activity, using market-based activities as a guide to how much care workers ought to be paid will be unreliable and likely unfair. Should wives who cook be paid as a chef or fry cook? Should competent mothers be paid more than incompetent mothers? There may be no coherent answer to these questions. Furthermore, it may not be a good idea to turn care work into a commodity because, as I argued in the last chapter, the commodification of some activities will destroy them.

We need to financially support care work without transforming it into a competitive market where the demands of efficiency threaten the internal goods of caring activity. Thus, facilitation for care workers—workplace flexibility, benefits, protection from discrimination, pay and benefits parity for part-time workers, limits on mandatory overtime, investment in daycare and eldercare infrastructure, and tax credits for caregivers—is more likely to be successful than direct compensation for many caregivers.

Beyond these family and care worker policies, any policy that minimizes uncertainty, anxiety, and fear is essential to maintaining conditions of social trust that enable people to act on their caring instincts. Thus, many liberal policy areas contribute to a care agenda, such as universal healthcare, a viable and secure economic safety net for everyone, accessible educational opportunities, and policies that enable immigrants, both legal and illegal, to become citizens. These policies will benefit society—they have the added benefit of reinforcing our self-understanding as caring individuals by making caring activity a dominant social norm.

CARING GLOBALLY

Conservatism and modern liberalism have always assumed international affairs are a Hobbesian world in which equally situated states pursue only their self-interest and agreements can be secure only when backed up by the credible threat of force.[2] Thus, conservatives argue that national security and the pursuit of national interest require the continual strategic use of military force. Peace can be achieved only through war. Modern liberals have endorsed the importance of military strength and have often used military force but are also committed to the possibility of reasonable states adopting universal principles of justice that can regulate relations between states as self-interested actors. States rationally assess their situation and understand that treating other states as free and equal partners warrants reciprocation, which is to everyone's benefit.

Though modern liberalism, with its policies of containing enemies and global institution building, has proven to be vastly superior to conservatism's perpetual war, neither has worked particularly well to preserve peace. The United States' failures in Iraq and Vietnam, the perpetual arms race that constantly threatens to metastasize into global nuclear conflict, and the new proposals for an open-ended war against terror show the futility of conservatism. Overwhelming military strength does not necessarily enable us to subdue people we disagree with, and war typically does not lead to peace or democracy. Even Hobbes recognized that peace required trust. His conservative followers fail to recognize that the barrel of a gun does not inspire trust. Conservatives forget that political authority flows from moral authority and that there is a vast difference between the exercise of power and the exercise of morally legitimate power. Nothing is more important to our security than the perception on the part of others that our policies are morally legitimate.

However, the liberal values of equality and liberty have not been a sufficient bulwark against excessive militarism. After all, the Vietnam War and the Iraq War, both fought for morally suspect reasons, had many liberal supporters. Modern liberalism is susceptible to the argument that if the values of liberty and equality are universal values, then we have the right to impose them on others since they must want them as well. It assumes that if others have not adopted liberal, democratic values it must be because they lack the freedom to choose—and we should use our weapons to give them the "choice."

But the question of what others want and what they are willing to do to get what they want cannot be answered a priori. Only a detailed, particular knowledge acquired through empathy and the perceptiveness of care will yield this kind of understanding. We are usually unwilling to listen attentively to others when the military option looks so inviting. Lack of this kind of knowledge played a significant role in the twin debacles of Iraq and Vietnam. In both cases, the United States made crucial mistakes about nationalist sentiment and the potential for protracted conflict that greater cultural knowledge might have avoided. An ethic of care, with its emphasis on empathy, tempers the tendency to assume that everyone shares our point of view.

Furthermore, our well-intentioned efforts to benefit the developing world, through both trade and direct aid, are hampered by moral assumptions built into modern liberalism. Just as many individuals are not free and equal and thus need care that is tailored to their unique situation, so many states are not free and equal either. Their power structure is the product of violence and fraud, their boundaries drawn arbitrarily by former colonial powers, their populations cowed by fear and debilitated by hunger and disease. Yet, we treat them as free and equal partners, entering into relationships of global exchange and diplomacy with vastly more powerful states that hold them accountable as if they had equal bargaining power and an institutional infrastructure that enables accountability and transparency.

The result is that much of the developing world never comes out ahead in these schemes. The foreign aid and profits they manage to acquire either find their way into the hands of corrupt oligarchs, who are granted legitimacy by the legal framework that governs global trade, or are recycled back into the coffers of global corporations because of mandates that development resources be purchased from preferred vendors. Again, part of the problem is that our needs are not their needs and our view of what their needs are is often not sensitive to local conditions.[3] Thus, our aid programs, like our military adventures, go awry. An ethic of care applied to development aid would institutionalize the kind of empathic approach needed to tailor aid to the real needs of recipients.

An ethic of care offers an alternative way of conceptualizing our relationships to other nations. It is built on the motives, reasons, and capacities that constitute healthy relationships. These include empathy, compassion, trust, and sensitivity regarding the particular characteristics of others and their situation. These motives and reasons are typically associated only with intimate relationships. But all relationships require sensitivity toward the vulnerabilities and particularities of others in order to generate trust, and relationships between nations and their people are no exception. Effective foreign policy requires the recognition that others are vulnerable in very particular ways and, if we are going to help them, we must respond to their vulnerability with empathy and perceptiveness that gives us insight into their situation.

The practices that prevent countries from developing are unjust, but the moral framework of modern liberalism is too thin to do much about it except offer up more agreements that assume the contractors to the agreement are free and equal. The ethics of care, by contrast, is able to articulate the interpersonal dimension of justice, the ways in which justice is dependent on a background of vulnerability and particularity that drives moral responsiveness. With its power and wealth, the United States can be a force of great good in the world, but only if it is not always promoting its own interests, looking at matters from its own perspective, or assuming illegitimately the universal perspective. We expect underdeveloped countries to drop their barriers to trade and open up their markets because economic nationalism threatens global trade. But if we are seen as self-interested and excessively nationalistic, we cannot expect others to refrain from their own destructive forms of economic nationalism.

With all this discussion of empathy, compassion, and trust, it is natural to think that the ethics of care is not sufficiently attuned to the threats that nations must confront and thus offers us no way of conceptualizing legitimate forms of self-defense. But there is nothing in the ethics of care that requires pacifism. The ethics of care takes special notice of circumstances when trust and the possibility of compassion and empathy do not exist. There is nothing fiercer than a mother protecting her children—care imposes on us requirements that we protect those we care about from danger. The flip side of care is passionate and powerful defense. But an ethic of care requires that we seek to preserve relationships, not destroy them, that we protect ourselves from monsters, not create and encourage them through an excess of aggression or machismo. The issue is not whether we should be assertive or accommodating in conducting foreign policy—we need to be both. The issue is preserving our moral authority when we act.

TRAGEDY OF THE COMMONS AND THE SOCIAL CONTRACT

Policies based on an ethic of care will help solve a variety of problems that the United States confronts. The defense of an ethic of care, however, needs a more general argument that explains why such a conception of ethics solves social problems. In this section I want to supply that argument by focusing on a challenge that will overwhelm us if we don't get the policies right—global warming. Preserving our human habitat has become a central function of government. In considering this greatest challenge, we get a clearer picture of why an ethic of care is necessary and how public and private institutions must be structured to implement it.

Our environment is best understood as part of the commons, which includes all the resources that we own collectively as citizens of a nation or as global inhabitants. Natural phenomena that do not lend themselves to private ownership such as the atmosphere, water supplies, or stocks of fish in the ocean are obvious examples.[4] These commons are under threat, which in turn threatens the very conditions of our survival. The global warming of the atmosphere, declining fish stocks and the health of oceans generally, and the depletion of natural resources, especially water supplies, show that the strategies we have used to protect the commons are not working and this calls into question the political ideologies and moral philosophies supporting those strategies.

Although the question of how to protect the commons harkens back to Thomas Malthus's infamous discussion of food supplies in the eighteenth century, much of the modern theoretical discussion was initiated by the biologist Garrett Hardin, who, in a paper titled "The Tragedy of the Commons," argued that the commons is under threat because individuals always have an incentive to exploit it rather than preserve it.[5] Hardin used the example of herdsmen grazing cattle in a common pasture. Each herdsman has reason to add more cows to increase his wealth, though the community would have to bear the cost of the new cow since it is grazing on the community's pasture. Because of this powerful incentive to graze more cows, eventually the pasture will reach the limit of its ability to feed the herd and will be destroyed. The herdsmen may know their habits are destructive, but, for each individual, there is no point in not adding more cattle since others are also going to use the pasture and it will be destroyed anyway. So even if everyone is aware of harm being done, selfishness and competitiveness will ruin the pasture. To update this example, we can substitute the earth's atmosphere for the common pasture and greenhouse gases, released by the burning of carbon-based fuels, for the cattle, and we have global warming as a tragedy of the commons. Each of us acting alone has an incentive to burn fossil fuels because refraining from doing so will be costly and would have little effect on overall CO_2 levels.

Hardin claimed there are only two solutions to the tragedy—allow the government to own and manage the common resource or allow private ownership of the resource. His preferred way of avoiding tragedy was to allow government ownership of the commons and impose strict regulations on who has access and how it is to be used. But selling off the commons to private interests may preserve it as well, he argued, since someone who owned a resource would preserve it for self-interested reasons.

The United States has employed a mixture of both strategies but the dominant trend, under increasingly conservative governance, has been to privatize as much of the commons as possible, and for those resources that cannot be owned privately, allow as much free access as possible. Today, almost anything that is sufficiently manageable to be sold in a market transaction is in private hands. Vast quantities of oil, minerals, public land, and other natural resources have been given over to private industry to exploit. Private industry has been allowed to exploit fish populations in the ocean with only minimal regulations. Airline routes, utilities, transportation systems, broadcast airwaves, and prisons have at least partly or wholly been placed under private ownership, as have many functions of the military. Even less tangible goods such as privacy and university research are now under the control of private corporations, and proposals for transferring more public goods into private hands are running apace. Proposals to give media corporations effective control over the Internet and to privatize Social Security have nearly passed in Congress, attempts to privatize public education abound, and proposals to protect biodiversity by selling access to plants and animals are seriously considered.[6]

The atmosphere that undergoes the chemical changes producing global warming cannot be corralled and placed in private hands. However, we have allowed private access to the atmosphere, allowing individuals to exploit it as they see fit, subject in recent years to some regulation of the pollutants introduced by that exploitation.

In many cases, privatizing goods or allowing free access has resulted in greater efficiency, lower prices, and wider distribution. Many goods can be more efficiently exploited by market mechanisms rather than public ownership. The problem is that privatization or free access does not guarantee that a resource is sustainable. The temptation to use up a resource in order to make a quick buck seems irresistible, especially when short-term profits and the ability to enter and exit a market quickly are the standards of success. The result is loss of the resource—the decline of fish stocks in the ocean is a prime example.

The alternative to privatization is the approach preferred by modern liberalism: give the resource to the government and provide proper incentives to cooperatively manage the resource, while using coercion when people cheat. But this approach has its problems. In mass societies, if there is no market to determine prices and bureaucracies must make production decisions, there is the constant danger of making costly resource allocation errors. Furthermore, in large, complex societies, it is hard to monitor compliance. Excessively authoritarian and intrusive forms of coercion must be used to make sure people cooperate. Thus, the dilemma we face is that, for a commons such as the atmosphere that cannot be privatized, free access leads to its destruction, but regulation is seen as coercive and it is difficult to get the public's consent for it.

The difficulties of resolving this dilemma are exacerbated by our political traditions that encourage assumptions that must be challenged if we are to find a solution. These assumptions are related to the fundamental idea of a social contract that guides our thinking about social and political questions. (See chapters 1 and 6 for more discussion.) In a culture guided by the idea of a social contract, each individual views her relationship to the commons as a strategic relationship that aims at her long-term advantage. Thus, her cooperation is always contingent on the cooperation of others, and she sees herself as obligated to sustain the commons only to the extent she is benefiting from the cooperation. This is the basic idea of the social contract—I'll scratch your back if you will scratch mine. But, since each individual is assumed to be self-interested, each of us wants the benefits of using the commons without the burdens of sustaining it, so each of us will try to avoid the burdens if we can. On the other hand, any hint of a free rider—someone who is not cooperating with the contract—encourages our defection from the contract since none of us want to be suckers. Thus, when enforcing the social contract, government regulations must be comprehensive and sanctions for not cooperating must be severe in order to discourage free riding. As noted above, the drawbacks of this approach are that comprehensive regulation runs the risk of overregulation and resource allocation mistakes in the absence of a market to determine supply and demand, severe sanctions cause great resentment even among those who cooperate, while weak sanctions allow free riders to prosper, which provides motivation for everyone to violate the contract.

This dilemma is a product of the conceptual limitations of social contract theory. Social contract theory encourages us to see formal, legal sanctions as the limit of moral engagement. To be a fully vested participant in the moral community, all one must do is obey the law for purely self-interested reasons. Thus, it does not give rise to the emotions of community. Instead, it encourages an "us against them" conception of government—government is useful only when I can take advantage of it. When it works to my disadvantage, I need only grudgingly acquiesce to its dictates until I can figure out a way to avoid sanctions for noncooperation. It is no wonder government has slipped into disrepute. Contract theory encourages it and conservatives, who wish to weaken regulations, take advantage of this. Given the assumptions of social contract theory, few people see the actions of government as an expression of their will. To the extent we see our relationship to the commons as a strategic relationship that aims only to serve self-interested motives, neither privatization nor government regulation will preserve it.

THE PRISONER'S DILEMMA AND AN ETHIC OF CARE

So what is the alternative? The alternative comes clearly into view when we treat the tragedy of the commons as a Prisoner's Dilemma. The Prisoner's Dilemma is a puzzle in game theory that illustrates the apparent conflict between what is rational for an individual to do versus what is best for the group as a whole. In its original formulation, it involves two players who are charged with a crime and must decide separately whether to confess to the police or remain silent. However, for our purposes, it is useful to look at choices that involve private versus public goods. The important constraint on conduct of the game is that all players are presumed to be thoroughly self-interested and rational.

Let's suppose we live in a car culture in which everyone drives cars with powerful, carbon-fuel based engines. I drive a gas-guzzling SUV and I know that spewing CO_2 into the environment causes global warming, which threatens our way of life. Should I purchase a less-desirable but less-polluting vehicle? If I believe that other drivers will not change their driving habits, then I have no reason to change mine, since eliminating the small amount of CO_2 that my vehicle contributes to global warming will have negligible effects on climate change. On the other hand, if I think most other drivers will change their driving habits, then it is still rational for me to continue to drive my SUV since the change in their driving habits will realize my goal of a stable climate, and I get to be a free rider. If everyone in this car culture follows the rational, self-interested strategy here, each player must conclude that she should continue to drive her gas guzzler. Thus, no one gets what we want—a stable climate.

The dilemma arises because all of us would prefer a stable climate, and we could satisfy our preferences if we cooperated. But cooperation appears to be irrational, if you don't know that other players will cooperate since you risk being a sucker, and irrational if you do know they will cooperate, since you can be a free rider and have your goal realized without your contribution. No matter what others do, it is rational to act in your self-interest. But, if each person is individually rational, cooperation is impossible and each person ends up with an outcome that she prefers less than another available outcome. The cooperative outcome (everyone driving low-emission vehicles) can be realized only if the players violate their self-interest.

Decisions about how society should allocate resources often have the structure of a Prisoner's Dilemma. The arms race, road congestion, air pollution, the depletion of fish stocks, and a variety of other commons, though each differs in detail, all have the structure of a Prisoner's Dilemma—it is individually rational for us to exploit and degrade these resources though we would prefer their sustainable use. Even goods such as education and public health can have the structure of a Prisoner's Dilemma. It is individually rational for us to seek lower taxes, though we would all prefer better education and public health that may require higher levels of taxation.

The good news is that we do manage to provide some social goods—our society is not an utter failure. This suggests that the Prisoner's Dilemma doesn't quite describe how actual human beings reason. The bad news is that our social and environmental systems are degraded enough to indicate that it describes our thinking at least some of the time. From arms races and street congestion to environmental pollution and the overexploitation of resources, we sometimes fail to realize our preferences because we fail to sufficiently commit ourselves to strategies of cooperation, just as the Prisoner's Dilemma predicts. Why?

One factor that might cause me to give up my SUV is that I might be punished or ostracized by others who are disturbed by my indifference toward the environment. The incentive to defect from cooperative arrangments is outweighed by the threat of punishment, thus allowing cooperation to emerge as the rational strategy. In fact, early computer simulations of Prisoner's Dilemma strategies, in which the game is repeated through many iterations, show that the most successful solution was the Tit-for-Tat strategy, in which an agent initially cooperates and then in future encounters responds in kind to an opponent's previous action.[7] In these simulated games, if a player cooperated in their previous interaction, the agent cooperates with that player. If that player did not cooperate in the past, the agent retaliates by declining to cooperate. According to the Tit-for-Tat strategy, it is rational for me to aquire a hybrid vehicle on a short-term lease. But if others do not make similar purchases, I should go back to driving my preferred vehicle.

This introduces reciprocal altruism into the picture and seems to capture the insight behind social contract theory. We cooperate when we have reason to believe our future interactions will matter, provided that others will cooperate as well. This helps explain why we are sometimes successful at providing social goods. In ordinary life, we usually interact with people over the long term and we need their approval and cooperation in the future. So it is in our long-term interests to cooperate with them. But if this models actual decision making, why are levels of social goods still inadequate?

Further computer simulations of the Prisoner's Dilemma help answer that question. In the standard Tit-for-Tat strategy, if I see others are not cooperating, I retaliate on the next move. But then others will retaliate in response to my noncooperation, thus causing a downward spiral of noncooperation that harms everyone. This strategy is especially counterproductive when communication is poor and players' moves are incorrectly reported or misunderstood—even when players intend to cooperate, mistakes will generate the downward spiral of noncooperation. This problem is exacerbated in real-life situations where players are actual human beings with tendencies toward irrationality. In our car culture, if I think others are not responding in a timely and comprehensive way to the threat of global warming, it is rational for me to go right back to driving my SUV, since the behavior of others leads me to think they are not cooperatng, though they may in fact be lazy, misinformed, too busy, and so on.

We see this consequence in countless instances in real life. Each side in a bargaining situation sees itself as cooperative as long as the other side cooperates. But each side feels forced to retaliate when, through miscommunication, misunderstanding, or a chance mishap, the other side fails to cooperate. Both sides are convinced they are in the right and the other side is simply evil. A wide range of phenomena from fighting in a school yard, to war between tribes or states, to failure to sustain resources, are explained by the belief that the people we are bargaining with are just irresponsible and unreasonable.

In the most recent simulations, the successful strategy in Prisoner's Dilemma tournaments employs a "nice" Tit-for-Tat strategy. The destructive cycle of retaliation is broken when players are willing to forgive the first defection. It pays to cooperate and forgive others at least once when they fail to cooperate. Thus, the negative effects of miscommunication and irrationality, which destroyed outcomes in the Tit-for-Tat strategy, are lessened to a degree. On the "nice" strategy, I don't immediately retaliate by driving the SUV but wait more patiently for the rest of society to come around.

Does the "nice" Tit-for-Tat strategy provide the conceptual basis for real-world solutions to cooperation problems? The problem is that miscommunication and misunderstanding are not occasional occurrences among human beings. Human beings routinely fail to communicate well, especially when under pressure. And we often succumb to various sorts of irrational behaviors. Hatred, fear, envy, and sheer lethargy, along with the self-deception that often accompanies them, are permanent elements of the human condition and they interfere with our ability to cooperate. In other words, we all appear to be persistent cheaters, and there is no reliable way of monitoring compliance in many situations. Thus, the opportunities for noncooperation to appear rational are pervasive in human life. In the real world, even a "nice" Tit-for-Tat strategy will all too often devolve into a war of all against all, overwhelmed by the sheer magnitude of our irrational tendencies. Self-interest with a limited capacity to forgive will be too unstable to accomplish significant cooperation.

Human survival requires a greater capacity for forgiveness and trust than even the "nice" strategy provides. This suggests that self-interested motives will never explain our capacity to cooperate and achieve our ends. If we were perfectly rational, effective communicators with transparent motives, perhaps we could generate cooperation out of purely self-interested motives—but we aren't and we can't.

This is where the motive and activity of care can make a contribution to our understanding of human behavior. The motive and activity of care uses the reservoir of social trust built up by our caring responses to build and sustain the capacity for additional caring responses. The motive and activity of care reduces fear and anger. It sustains a basis for cooperation even in the face of miscommunication and irrationality, because it rests on unconditional generosity that suppresses the propensity to defect and encourages others to respond with care as well. The motive of care encourages persistence regarding what we care about; despite the fact that other drivers remain committed to their gas-guzzlers and despite the fact that my action has little effect on global warming, I should persist in driving a hybrid vehicle.

Why is this rational? It is rational to want one's actions to conform to one's moral identity. If I care deeply enough about preserving a stable climate, then having a coherent self-concept requires that my actions conform to my ideals. The responsibility lies with each individual to manage their own motives in light of what they care about. Granted, the goal of mitigating global warming involves large-scale collective responses to energy needs over which I have little control, but in the end it is my responsibility to respond to the moral address of those with whom I am in relationship (the face of the Other) and to sustain the motives that enable me to respond to their needs. It involves no great leap of imagination to see in my child's face the face of his children, to see in my neighbor's face the face of his neighbor, and to realize that only through the sustained commitment of one's character to their needs will my response to their command be adequate. The Prisoner's Dilemma is a dilemma only because it assumes that moral rationality must aim at bringing about a state of affairs—in this case a stable climate. My actions alone cannot do that; but neither do they aim at that outcome. They aim at responding to the face; they are rational because they make agency possible. (See chapter 8.) We solve Prisoner's Dilemma–type problems when we view a certain action as a matter of personal integrity and moral responsibility regardless of outcome.

However, individuals acting alone with integrity will not solve the global warming crisis. A collective, institutional commitment is necessary, and this discussion of the Prisoner's Dilemma suggests the shape of that commitment. Approximately 85 percent of the energy used by the world's economy is derived from fossil fuels.[8] According to the Intergovernmental Panel on Climate Change, in order to stabilize the greenhouse gas concentration at 2000 levels, a level at which the worst risks would be reasonably unlikely, global emissions would have to be reduced by more than 50 percent below present levels by the year 2050.[9]

Reductions at this level will require enormous sacrifices, and there are many reasons to be skeptical about our ability to make them. (1) The sacrifices may not yield any immediate, palpable, compensating benefits aside from avoiding the destruction of our habitat. Since we cannot experience what does not occur, avoiding a loss is never as satisfying as achieving a gain, and the economic costs may seem to be too much to bear. (2) The current generation will suffer less from global warming than future generations and the present generation need not fear reprisals from future generations since we won't be around to experience the recriminations. Thus, current generations have a powerful self-interested reason to continue emitting CO_2. (3) Developing nations have few resources to combat global warming, and many will be loathe to implement policies that might force them to sacrifice economic growth and cause them to slide back into poverty. (4) The two main proposals on the table for confronting global warming—a carbon tax or a cap and trade system—are easily gamed and considerations of fairness will require complex and intrusive regulatory systems, which encourage defection.

Given these obstacles, it is obvious that no Tit-for-Tat strategy ("nice" or otherwise) will sustain a commitment to ending our dependence on fossil fuels. The incentives to defect from cooperative arrangements will overwhelm our efforts if our actions are contingent on the actions of others. We cannot afford to refuse to act if we are dissatisfied with the lack of short-term compensating benefit, and we cannot take the absence of an advocate for future generations as a license to exploit their interests. Furthermore, we cannot respond to the refusal of other nations to cooperate by withdrawing our cooperation. If the United States and other developed nations wait to get commitments from developing nations before committing to reduce their own use of fossil fuels—which was the United States' policy toward the Kyoto Protocol and a major reason why the protocols were ineffective—climate change will accelerate. And we will have to be vigilant and disciplined over the long term in order to avoid the corruption of the regulatory system needed to defend against this threat.

We can overcome these obstacles only by extending generosity to future generations and developing nations while refusing to allow cheaters to deflect us from our commitment. The solution to the Prisoner's Dilemma suggests that we will have to make the first move, be consistent in our commitment to substantial reductions in greenhouse gases, and be generous in distributing technology, while applying sanctions judiciously when they are likely to cause compliance rather than retaliation. Success will come only through building trust and maintaining the moral authority that comes from maintaining the integrity of our motives. The United States and Europe will have to lead from an ethic of care in order to get the job done.

Of course, this generosity must have limits. The free rider must be prevented from running roughshod over agreements and undermining the social trust on which the agreements rest. Holding people responsible is an essential component of the second-personal competence at work in responding to the face of the Other. The existence of free riders is a trade-off—it is the cost of doing business in a large, free society where monitoring compliance is costly or impossible. But compliance is more likely when generosity is viewed as the norm. It is easy to lack gratitude when the rest of society is indifferent. It takes a special kind of sociopath to live without gratitude in a culture of care.

If dispositions to care are required to explain cooperation, then it is implausible to maintain the assumption that unadulterated, rational self-interest is our most fundamental motivation. Yet this is the assumption on which much of modern social and political theory rests and that an ethic of care disputes. Our ability to cooperate and solve problems is limited by our mistaken self-understanding, encouraged by our intellectual traditions, that views caring responses as irrational, private matters inappropriate in the rough-and-tumble world of economics and politics.

A CARING ECONOMY

How do we get our institutions that have arisen against the backdrop of these mistaken assumptions about human nature to embody an ethic of care and responsibility? An important first step to institutionalizing an ethic of care and responsibility is to see economic markets not as impersonal forces governed by natural laws, but as a system of relationships that need trust and support. *Genuinely* free economic markets are not the enemy. They are essential to an ethic of care and responsibility because they express our interdependence, take the uniqueness of individuals seriously, prevent concentrations of power that inhibit the acceptance of responsibility, and generate enormous wealth that can be used to ameliorate human suffering.

Rootstock liberalism does not reject free markets but recognizes them as human creations that are used to satisfy a particular constellation of interests. The creation and maintenance of markets requires a variety of decisions by various social and political actors that determine the shape of a market; and it matters crucially whether these decisions are well made and who makes them.

Through the influence of campaign donations and the use of lobbyists to write legislation, big business has created the rules that govern markets and manage the oversight function of government in a way that undermines free markets. The upshot is plutocracy—an economy and culture controlled by a few elites who rig the game so they always come out on top, resulting in advancing inequalities that prevent people from fully participating in American life, and perpetuating this peculiar moral regime of independent/economic man as an ideology because it is good for the bottom line.

Free markets do not inevitably lead to the exploitation of workers, consumers, or the environment. But they will if the market system operates in a culture in which independent man and economic man have the upper hand. Maximal efficiency and juvenile freedom is a toxic mix that unleashes inhuman motives when not called to account. They exploit trends in which many market transactions no longer involve face-to-face interaction, where honesty, integrity, and respect can be more easily assessed and lay the foundation of social trust.

This is the heart of the problem with contemporary capitalism. Because of the mobility of capital in a global market, the modern cor-

However, government regulation is inherently problematic and by itself cannot succeed in giving capitalism a human face. Oversight and regulation often result in cumbersome bureaucratic procedures that inhibit innovation, intrude unnecessarily in the lives of individuals, and kill the spontaneous ability of people to work together. Government regulation means that many decisions will be based on political interests rather than market forces. And political outcomes will often represent the power and interests of their proponents rather than the common good, resulting in serious resource allocation mistakes.

Furthermore, business now operates in a global environment, where no government has the ability to impose its will, and in a volatile, competitive atmosphere that requires constant innovation and the ability to respond rapidly to changes in the business environment. But government regulation is often inflexible, slow to change, and thus will stifle innovation; the threat of punishment will never adequately motivate moral agents to meet their obligations. Government regulation has an important role to play but one that is limited by the problems inherent with political decision making and authoritarian enforcement.

None of the challenges we face as a country can be met without government. One of the great tasks of progressive liberalism is to find more-efficient and effective methods of government oversight and accountability. But relying on oversight alone is a characteristic of the liberalism of the past and it is likely to run into the same impediments that brought about its demise. A progressive liberalism must seek out new ways of enabling the coordination and cooperation at which government regulation aims, without the side effects. But, in addition to reasonable regulations and enforcement mechanisms, the moral priorities of all stakeholders—management, stockholders, employees, customers, and the public—must be in alignment. A sense of obligation that arises from within the organization is superior to one imposed from the outside by government.

Thus, a second approach to encouraging corporate responsibility and ethical decision-making attempts to align the motives of stakeholders through the profit motive. If stockholders, consumers, and employees prefer to deal only with companies that are socially responsible and ethically aware, then in order to preserve profit margins, corporations will have to include moral calculations in their business decisions. Their aim will still be to maximize profit, but they will realize that business ethics and social responsibility are the means to achieve profitability because consumers and other stakeholders will insist on it. In fact, today there are many businesses that view social responsibility as a source of profit—the organic food movement, the commitment some companies have made to minimize their carbon footprint, or the avoidance of sweatshop labor are examples of profitability based on what stakeholders want.

However, there are difficulties in relying on consumers to bring about capitalism with a human face. This model depends crucially on consumers having the information to make informed decisions. But corporations control much of that information and possess vast resources to shape public perceptions, lobby government, and defend themselves in court against allegations of wrongdoing. It is not obvious that consumers have the information or legal and political clout to force the necessary changes in business practices. Furthermore, ethical consumers have inherent conflicts of interest—we work for and invest in the very firms we are trying to change through purchasing decisions, and any constraints on profit will feed back negatively on consumers and investors. These are all reasons to think that the impact of consumer activism may be uneven and that companies that take corporate responsibility seriously will put themselves at a competitive disadvantage because competitors will not all be playing by the same rules, an important and potentially fatal disincentive for business ethics.

The third alternative is to fundamentally reconceptualize our notion of the corporation. Since its creation in the late nineteenth century, the corporation has been understood as a private entity owned by stockholders and governed by a single purpose—to generate profits for shareholders. But today, there is little justification for thinking of most corporations as private entities, no justification for thinking of shareholders as owners of the corporation, and no reason to think that profit should be the sole aim of the corporation.

Corporations were given legal rights on the condition that they serve society and, by their very nature, they are dependent on the physical and moral infrastructure of society and the public affirmation of their role expressed through the law. Thus, they have a public purpose. Furthermore, they lack the zone of privacy that persons enjoy since they lack the capacity for consciousness. They are fundamentally not private entities at all.

Neither does the concept of private property give us a handle on the nature of the corporation. Corporations are no longer made up of parcels that can be fenced off from society. Most businesses today are made up of assets that are not physical objects but are intangible, relational goods—brand loyalties, the public reputation that secures brand loyalty, ongoing research projects with a variety of independent actors, networks of people that form complex supply chains and information flows, and most important, the knowledge and abilities of employees, managers, and consultants. A business does not own the skills, ability, experience, or relationships of the people who make it up because these sorts of things cannot be owned—the best that business can do is contract for their temporary and conditional use, which can be withdrawn at anytime.

Moreover, shareholders do not qualify as owners of property rights. They share nothing tangible—they simply have transferable contractual rights to a share of a company's product. Since the late nineteenth century, legal norms have separated the holding of shares from ownership of corporate assets. A shareholder cannot march into a corporate office and demand their coffee machine. And given limited liability and the ability to diversify holdings, investing in shares of a company is no longer particularly risky. The historical record shows that most stocks are relatively low-risk investments with substantial returns in the long run. Shareholders now routinely receive dividends from their shares and hold diversified portfolios. Thus, shares are sources of steady income. Shareholders are not speculative adventurers whose returns will shift dramatically with the fortunes of a single company. They are passive investors who without effort, talent, or substantial risk enjoy enormous gains from profitable companies. Yet, despite these conceptual problems, we still operate under the illusion that shareholders are owners, and therefore, management has the fiduciary duty to maximize their profit.

If corporations are not parcels of private property, then what are they? Perhaps, we should conceive of the corporation as a productive community that must encompass the interests of a wide range of stakeholders—investors, employees, suppliers, customers, and management. A community is a group of people governed by collective intentions important enough to induce a sense of identity and cohesiveness among its members. A corporation satisfies this definition if the stakeholders share a purpose.

What then is the purpose of the corporation? If it is simply to make a profit for the shareholders, there may not be enough shared interest among all stakeholders to qualify as a single purpose. But given that shareholders are not owners, there is no reason to impose this conception of a purpose on corporations. An analysis of a free market transaction gives us a clue as to the purpose of a corporation. When one uncoerced agent sells an item to another uncoerced agent for a price, both end up in a situation with more value than their pretransaction position. If I purchase a car from the car dealer for $20,000, then I must want the car more than the $20,000 and the dealer wants the $20,000 more than the car. As a result of the transaction, value has been created. Both of us through this transaction now have something we didn't have before. This is the very heart of the theory of capitalism. Market transactions create value for everyone involved (assuming the externalities have been captured in the price). However, this suggests that the purpose of free market transactions is to create value, to create something that did not exist before. Profit, of course, is a kind of value. Presumably the car dealer made a profit on her transaction. But there are other values created by the transaction as well. A variety of human needs are taken care of including my need for a car, the salesperson's need for a salary or commission, and the community's need for mobile citizens.

Theorists of capitalism have always made much of the claim that in this transaction there was no intention to improve the welfare of society. No shared goal explains how the transaction added value. I do not intend the car salesperson's good; she does not intend mine. We are thoroughly self-interested in the transaction; there is no moral aim here, only an invisible hand dispensing distributive justice. But defenders of free market capitalism (and the invisible hand) typically ignore the fact that the value created by this transaction presupposes a variety of collective intentions that must already exist in order for the transaction to take place. Individual transactions do not require collective intentions but the institutions that enable the transaction clearly do.

Most goods and services require labor to produce them, and this labor requires the exercise of abilities and capacities that reside in individuals. But these individual abilities and their productive use depend on a social process in which the abilities are recognized and appropriated through knowledge and know-how, which are social goods because they cannot be possessed solely by individuals. The processes through which we identify human needs and acquire the skills, capacities, and knowledge required to satisfy those needs, and the implicit agreements required to organize production, are part of this process of creating value, and these are thoroughly social processes, not owned by anyone in particular. Thus, it is not just the employee's time and ability that is being purchased by management, neither is it only the shareholder's risk, or management's expertise that is being exploited. Management is tapping into and exploiting a vast and very deep social network that enables any simple commodity exchange.

The product is assigned a kind of abstract value through market transactions that give us a rough understanding of its value. But the product's value is not just in the satisfaction of a consumer's prefer- ence measured as a reflection of what someone will pay for it. Before it is exchanged, the product is already infused with value. The price of the product—its exchange value—is a practical device for estab- lishing equivalences between vastly different products and it is enor- mously useful in that it helps us avoid allocation mistakes so we don't end up producing something no one wants. Money, and the exchange it enables, is not the root of evil. But it reflects only a part of what that production and service really is; and there is nothing invisible about this process unless one refuses to look.

The corporation gathers together this social network. It is a pro- ductive community whose aim is to satisfy the needs and wants that are essential to our attempts to live well. To the degree we reduce this goal to the simple accumulation of profit, we fundamentally misun- derstand its purpose. Of course, there are different constituencies within the corporation whose interests will diverge from time to time. And all constituents must be cognizant of the importance of profit and shareholder value. But profit is the instrument that enables the satisfaction of needs and wants—not the ultimate goal.

The corporation was created because it is a value-creating

machine. The aim of creating value is a motive that all stakeholders can share; it is the source of the robust collective intentions that make corporations successful because the interests of everyone are aligned at a general level.[10] Each person sees her self-interest as instrumental in creating the output of the corporation. A corporation organized around this motive would not be a person, but it would unleash the second personal competence (which includes recognition of the face of the Other) in its people by providing a purpose that all stake-holders share, the creation of value. The upshot is an organization built on mutual trust between stakeholders who share a goal.[11]

The worry about this conception of the corporation is that the competitive demands of the marketplace will shape the norms of such a community so that the higher purpose becomes an empty slogan masking a more fundamental drive for profit. It is anything but clear what policies we should adopt to make this vision of the corporation a reality. But it is perhaps one of the most important intellectual tasks of contemporary liberalism to find this path from here to there.

THE POLITICS OF CARE

Alexis de Tocqueville, in his insightful nineteenth-century description of the United States, distinguished two kinds of patriotism:

> There is one sort of patriotic attachment which principally arises from that instinctive, disinterested, and undefinable feeling which connects the affections of man with his birthplace. This natural fondness is united with a taste for ancient customs and a reverence for traditions of the past; those who cherish it love their country as they love the mansion of their fathers. . . . It is in itself a kind of religion: it does not reason, but it acts from the impulse of faith and sentiment. In some nations the monarch is regarded as a personification of the country; and, the fervor of patriotism being converted into the fervor of loyalty, they take a sympathetic pride in his conquests, and glory in his power.[12]

Tocqueville admired this patriotism for its passion in the short run but thought it was unlikely to endure. But in the United States he observed a different kind of patriotism at work:

A man comprehends the influence which the well-being of his country has upon his own; he is aware that the laws permit him to contribute to that prosperity, and he labors to promote it, first because it benefits him, and secondly because it is in part his own work. . . . [H]ow does it happen that everyone takes as zealous an interest in the affairs of his township, his county, and the whole state as if they were his own? It is because everyone, in his sphere, takes an active part in the government of society.[13]

I fear that over the past half-century we have lost this second, distinctively American form of patriotism and have reverted to some version of the first. Too many Americans exult in bombing small countries to smithereens, yell self-righteous approval when an ignorant president thumbs his nose at the rest of the world, gloat approvingly when the moral superiority of all things American is asserted, and take pride in our plundering of the world's resources—a patriotic fervor whipped up solely from the thrill of being connected to power.

That second, distinctly American form of patriotism, which Tocqueville describes, demands more of each of us. It requires a commitment to nurture our public life, a commitment that has not been in evidence in recent years. It speaks volumes that when President Bush took to the podium to rally Americans to the cause of his "war on terror," we were not enjoined to sacrifice, to learn, or to become engaged citizens—he implored us to go shopping and support his massive tax cuts for the wealthy.

The engaged patriotism that Tocqueville admired has receded because it requires a simple insight that is, all too often, beyond our grasp: my welfare depends on the welfare of others. I am healthier when those around me are healthy; I am better educated when those around me are educated; I am wealthy when those around me are wealthy. There is nothing particularly profound in this idea—it is a common sentiment. But it too often remains merely a sentiment because the modern world and our political traditions keep it under wraps. As the world becomes more complex and more integrated and the threads of our lives more entangled in knots of untraceable crossings, we need greater moral insight and moral commitment in order to keep the simple truth of our mutual dependence in view. We need a political movement that takes up this insight as its cause.

The family is the best example of how a sense of mutual dependence and responsibility produces cooperation. The family has evolved as the fundamental social unit of society, not because it has some particular structure or because it is the bearer of traditions, but because it rests on unconditional generosity, which takes mistrust off the table, thus enabling an extraordinary degree of cooperation. In well-functioning families trust is simply assumed, motives to defect are discounted, and forgiveness is routine. Our lives are enabled as a result.

Of course within families, feelings of affection encourage this unconditional generosity. But affection is not necessary for generosity; most of us have family members for which we would sacrifice even though we may not feel affection for them. Moreover, outside the family there are examples of routine generosity that characterize our lives despite the absence of feelings of affection. We obey the law even when the cops are not around. People give blood, vote even when they cannot influence an election, donate time to developing free software or to disseminate free information on the Internet, devote time to comforting strangers in distress, allow others to cut ahead in line, give directions, give money and volunteer time to charity, take care of a neighbor's house while she's on vacation, and go out of our way to help coworkers on the job even when we could get away with less expenditure of time, energy, or money. This side of our nature is an untapped resource; it can no longer be understood merely as a private, idiosyncratic response to human need.

The arguments in this book show that the opposition between self-interest and altruism, on which our political traditions rest, is a false dilemma. The motive to care is not devoid of self-interest but instead collapses the opposition between my interests and the interests of others. Care requires the perception that my interests and the interests of others are inextricably intertwined. As social beings we grant others the right to make claims on us—a bounded yet unconditional response to the vulnerability of others that provides structure to our interactions. The gratuitous act of generosity in responding to human vulnerability is central to human cooperation. If we are able to solve the many problems that belabor us, it will be because we recognize and internalize this.

It will take a new kind of politics to acquire this revised self-understanding. But it cannot be a politics that relies exclusively on establishment politicians and their advisors. I have been arguing for a public philosophy that requires a transformation in personal morality. But governments and the politicians who manage them are not the proper agents of this transformation. This can come only from people themselves. Despite conservatism's rants about the battle against evil, it is not the responsibility of government to transform the soul, although government can help make moral commitment more likely. Neither does the responsibility for change fall on one segment of society or some particular institution—the corporate CEO as well as the single mother can practice an ethic of care. Rootstock liberalism is a movement of grassroots and netroots, of boardrooms and bedrooms, of union halls and the halls of Congress. When individuals change, institutions change as well.

It might be argued that a political movement based on an ethics of care would lack the proper motives for engaging in the kind of bruising political fight that can win elections. Indeed, an ethics of care emphasizes compassion, trust, and generosity; but, as I noted above, it is acutely aware of when the conditions for compassion, trust, and generosity do not exist. Care is a motive for combat when what we care about is threatened; and if anything is worth fighting for, it is our relationships. Tough, negative campaigning that refuses to back down in the face of the lies and deceptions of right-wing politics is no less ethical than attacking someone who is harming your children. American voters have elected conservatives, despite their cruelty and ignorance, because they advertise their toughness and backbone. Liberalism must show a different sort of backbone—a commitment to improving the human condition that does not waver.

The election of Barack Obama to the presidency gives us hope that such a commitment might anchor our public policy. As of this writing, it is too early to know if this hope is misplaced. However, his rhetoric calls us to a higher purpose by recognizing that our destiny as Americans is bound up with one another; and his campaign organization was based, in part, on a commitment to grassroots support that beckons ordinary people to take their government back from the plutocrats that have nearly destroyed our nation. The task of building a culture of care seems to follow straightforwardly. Rootstock liberalism is a kind of identity politics because it places the self-understanding of a liberal person with specific moral virtues at the heart of its ideology. But it is not an identity politics based on race, ethnicity, or gender. Identity—a person's understanding of her essential characteristics—is defined by moral commitments, the people and activities about which one cares, and one's capacity to respond to the vulnerability and particularity of others. Rootstock liberalism names a politics that seeks to build institutions and practices that strengthen those commitments and that keeps before us the simple thought that one's own happiness is dependent on the happiness of others. Thus, rootstock liberalism is not an identity politics of exclusion because all of us are vulnerable particulars. It welcomes the face of anyone it encounters because our existence depends on that welcome.

Identity politics is not new to American political culture. The Republican Party's attacks on liberals have always relied on the implicit understanding that liberals are not true Americans—they are too secular, too academic, too foreign in their tastes, too accommodating to people who are not like us, lacking the confident assertiveness to have our way with the world. Democrats too have been accused of identity politics, promoting the interests of minority groups that see themselves as oppressed because of their marginalized identities.

Both versions of identity politics are un-American. Our nation was founded on the promise that a political association need not be based on bloodlines, mythologies of origin, or religion but on the ability of citizens to come to agreement about how to conduct our public life. A commitment to care for the quality of that public life is our national identity. To be a real American is to make that commitment.

ENDNOTES

INTRODUCTION

1. For polling regarding political trends, see "Trends in Political Values and Core Attitudes, 1987–2007," Pew Research Center for People and the Press, March 27, 2007, http://people-press.org/report/?reportid=312 (accessed June 18, 2007).

2. The victory of Proposition 8 in California, which writes prohibitions on gay marriage into the state constitution in a state that voted overwhelmingly for Obama, shows that short-term liberal voting patterns can coexist with conservative moral intuitions.

3. According to the Harris Poll, in 1970, 49 percent of adults identified themselves as Democrats. By 2003, Democratic self-identifiers had shrunk to 33 percent of the electorate. During that time, Independents and those who did not identify with either party increased substantially while the percentage of Republican self-identifiers remained comparatively consistent.

4. For a summary of these data, see Christopher Muste, "Hidden in Plain Sight: Polling Data Show Moral Values Aren't a New Factor," *Washington Post*, December 12, 2004, p. B4.

5. John Gastil, Dan M. Kahan, and Donald Braman, "Ending Polarization: The Good News about the Culture Wars," *Boston Review*, March/April, 2006.

6. According to Pew Research in November of 2008, only 21 percent of Americans call themselves liberal; 38 percent say they are conservative, and 36 percent describe themselves as moderate. These percentages have been relatively stable. In 2000, at the beginning of the Bush administration, 18 percent of Americans said they were liberal, 36 percent were conservative, and 38 percent considered themselves moderate. See Juliana Horowitz, "Winds of Political Change Haven't Shifted Public's Ideology Balance," Pew Research Center for People and the Press, November 25, 2008.

7. See Mark Danner, "How Bush Won," *New York Review of Books* 52, no. 1, January 13, 2005. The candidacies of Michael Dukakis in 1988 and Al Gore in 2000 were similarly damaged by the perception that they lacked strength of character. Bill Clinton's presidency was dogged by wild accusations of corruption, murder, and treason, although he had the political skills to overcome them.

8. James Carville, Stanley Greenberg, and Robert Shrum, "Toward a Democratic Purpose," Democracy Corps Survey, February 1, 2005, http://www.gqrr.com/index.php?ID=1224 (accessed June 18, 2007).

CHAPTER 1

1. President George W. Bush, "Second Inaugural Address," Thursday, January 20, 2005. See Bartleby's *Inaugural Addresses of the Presidents of the United States*, Bartleby.com, http://www.bartleby.com/124/pres67.html (accessed June 28, 2008).

2. President George W. Bush, "Prayer Service Remarks," National Day of Prayer and Remembrance for the Victims of the Terrorist Attacks, September 11, 2001, at Washington National Cathedral, September 14, 2001. Transcript is available at US Office of Personnel Management, http://www.opm.gov/guidance/09-14-01gwb.htm (accessed June 28, 2008).

3. See Sean Hannity, *Deliver Us from Evil: Defeating Terrorism, Despotism, and Liberalism* (New York: Harper Paperbacks, 2005), and David Frum and Richard Pearle, *An End to Evil: How to Win the War on Terror* (New York: Ballantine Books, 2004).

4. A transcript of Ronald Reagan's speech at the 1964 Republican Convention is available at the Reagan Information Page, http://www.president reagan.info/speeches/the_speech.cfm (accessed June 28, 2008).

5. Quoted in Richard Hofstadter, *The Paranoid Style in American Politics and Other Essays* (New York: Knopf, 1966), p. 116.

6. Barry Goldwater, *The Conscience of a Conservative* (Princeton, NJ: Princeton University Press, 2007), p. 18.

7. Patrick J. Buchanan, "Republican National Convention Speech," August 17, 1992, http://www.buchanan.org/pa-92-0817-rnc.html (accessed June 29, 2008).

8. This criticism of contemporary values is common fare among conservatives. Perhaps the clearest formulation of this critique is in Gertrude Himmelfarb, *One Nation, Two Cultures* (New York: Vintage Books, 1999). See also William J. Bennett, *The Devaluing of America* (Focus on the Family Publications, 1994) and Robert Bork, *Slouching toward Gomorrah: Modern Liberalism and American Decline* (New York: HarperCollins, 2003). Himmelfarb does not employ the rhetoric of evil but she describes conservatism's battle against moral decay in Manichean, world-historical terms.

9. For an account of self-reliance as the primary mechanism of moral improvement, see David Frum, *Dead Right* (New York: Basic Books, 1994).

10. For a discussion of the cognitive roots of the importance of authority for conservatism, especially in the family, see George Lakoff, *Moral Politics: How Liberals and Conservatives Think*, 2nd ed. (Chicago: University of Chicago Press, 1996): pp. 65–107.

CHAPTER 2

1. See especially, Daniel Bell, *The Cultural Contradictions of Capitalism* (New York: HarperCollins, 1996).

2. Conservative intellectuals in the Burkean tradition are not opposed to all development and do not view any particular tradition as having absolute authority. Burke argued that change must be an organic, cultural development rather than imposed on society by elites. Contemporary philosophers associated with conservatism, such as John Kekes and Alistair MacIntyre, attempt to explain how change occurs organically and permit a good deal of pluralism in their visions of a community. However, the contemporary conservative political movement is less subtle in their deployment of traditional values as absolute, fixed guidelines, especially on domestic policy and the family. With the exception of some libertarians, the writings of William Buckley, William Bennett, and Gertrude Himmelfarb as well as conservative Christians reflect the idea of a tradition as having absolute authority. It is less clear that tradition plays the same role in conservative foreign policy. There is a good deal of debate within conservatism about whether the aggressive, idealistic, and heroic vision of American world domination that one finds in neoconservatism is compatible with the pragmatic humility expressed by Burke. But as I argued in chapter 1, the idea of American Exceptionalism is a well-rehearsed tradition that has driven American foreign policy at least since Teddy Roosevelt.

3. For the conservative argument regarding the slippery slope to polygamy, see Charles Krauthammer, "Beyond Gay Marriage," *Washington Post*, March 17, 2006, and Stanley Kurtz, "The Road to Polygamy," *Weekly Standard*, August 4, 2003.

4. For a recent version of this argument, see Lee Harris, "The Future of Tradition," *Policy Review*, June 2005. See also James Q. Wilson, *The Moral Sense* (New York: Free Press, 1993).

5. Eliot Turiel, *The Culture of Morality* (New York: Cambridge University Press, 2002).

6. For a brief account of Republican leadership's use of religion to justify corruption, see Joe Conason, "Let Us Prey," *Salon.com*, January 6, 2006.

CHAPTER 3

1. See Clarence Thomas, "Personal Responsibility," *Regent University Law Review* (Fall 1999).

2. Myron Magnet, "What Is Compassionate Conservatism?" *Wall Street Journal*, February 5, 1999.

3. The seminal work advocating self-reliance as a mechanism of moral improvement was Charles Murray, *Losing Ground: American Social Policy 1950–1980* (New York: Basic Books, 1984).

4. David Frum, *Dead Right* (New York: Basic Books, 1994), p. 4.

5. The average forty-year-old male made about $46,000 in 1973 (in current dollars). In 2005, he made approximately $41,000 despite the fact that the American economy had nearly doubled on a per-person basis. Women have made more impressive advances as more have entered the workforce, though their pay still lags behind men. Statistics from US Census Bureau, Housing and Household Economics Statistics Division, http://www.census.gov/hhes/www/income/histinc/p08ar.html (accessed April 28, 2008). For a statistical survey of these economic trends, see Lawrence Mishel, Jared Bernstein, and Sylvia Allegretto, *The State of Working America* (Ithaca, NY: Cornell ILR Press, 2006).

6. Michael Ledeen, *The War against the Terror Masters* (New York: St. Martin's Griffin, 2003), pp. 212–13.

7. For research in sociology on these phenomena, see Richard Sennett, *The Culture of the New Capitalism* (New Haven, CT: Yale University Press, 2006).

8. For a comprehensive account of this risk shift as an intentional policy, see Jacob Hacker, *The Great Risk Shift: The Assault on American Jobs, Fam-*

ilies, Health Care and Retirement—and How You Can Fight Back (New York: Oxford University Press, 2006).

9. For a defense of this view of moral hazard and health insurance, see *Economic Report of the President*, 2004, chapter 10, http://a257.g .akamaitech.net/7/257/2422/20feb20041530/www.gpoaccess.gov /usbudget/fy05/pdf/2004_erp.pdf (accessed June 4, 2008). As far as I know, this theory of moral hazard applied to healthcare was first advanced by Mark Pauly, "The Economics of Moral Hazard: Comment," *American Economic Review* 58 (1968): 531–37.

10. Comprehensive data for the No Child Left Behind Act, which was passed in 2002, are only beginning to be collected. Recent data suggest these hypotheses about No Child Left Behind will be confirmed. For the claim that NCLB is narrowing the curriculum and causing teachers to teach to the test, see the report by Jennifer McMurrer for Center on Education Policy, "Choices, Changes, and Challenges: Curriculum and Instruction in the NCLB Era," http://www.cep-dc.org/index.cfm?fuseaction=document .showDocumentByID&nodeID=1&DocumentID=212 (accessed April 20, 2008). See also James Ryan, "Perverse Incentives of No Child Left Behind Act," *New York University Law Review* (June 2004). A new report by Linda Valli at the University of Maryland's College of Education finds that high-stakes testing undermines teaching quality; see Linda Valli, *Test-Driven: High Stakes Accountability in Elementary Schools* (New York: Teachers College Press, 2008).

11. We are in fact seeing this policy being implemented. According to an Associated Press report of February 26, 2007, from 2003 to 2006 there were 12 percent less FDA employees in field offices who concentrated on food issues. Safety tests for food produced in the United States dropped nearly 75 percent, from 9,748 in 2003 to 2,455 last year, according to the agency's own statistics, even as imports from China and other countries were growing by leaps and bounds. And under Bush administration rules, when the FDA finds a problem, compliance by the company is typically voluntary. See http:// www.msnbc.msn.com/id/17349427/ (accessed June 30, 2008).

12. A recent study comparing countries where abortion is legal and countries where abortion is restricted found that legal sanctions had no influence on a woman's decision to have an abortion. But the legal status of abortion did affect how dangerous the procedure was. In countries where abortion was legal it was generally a safe procedure; in countries where abortion was illegal it was more likely to be performed under unsafe conditions by poorly trained providers. See Dr. Gilda Sedgh et al., "Induced Abortion: Estimated Rates and Trends Worldwide," *Lancet* 370 (October 13, 2007): 1338–45.

13. Conservatives will often cite the Personal Responsibility and Work Opportunity Reconciliation Act of 1996 as an example of how cracking down on scofflaws improves behavior. The aim of this legislation was to end dependence on welfare by putting a time limit on benefits. A study by the Urban Institute calls that into question. Shortly after the act was enacted, 31 percent of welfare recipients had found some work in the previous twelve months. By 2002, that percentage had increased to 37 percent—a very modest improvement. But in 2002, 20 percent of welfare recipients had no job and no cash welfare, most of them poor single mothers who were made much worse off by the reform. And former welfare recipients who were working had a median wage of about eight dollars per hour. This is hardly a ringing endorsement of the claim that knocking people around makes them better. See Urban Institute, "A Decade of Welfare Reform: Facts and Figures," June 2006, http://www.urban.org/publications/900980.html (accessed April 28, 2008).

14. Aristotle viewed self-sufficiency as a virtue at least for the contemplative individual. I depart from Aristotle's analysis on this point.

15. It is important to note that wealth in and of itself does not undermine our interest in morality. In fact, economic growth is essential to avoiding resentments that lead to hostile attitudes, excessive competitiveness, and so on. When the pie shrinks we are much more likely to fight over the size of the pieces. We are more likely to be tolerant, welcoming, and solicitous when our incomes are growing. For empirical evidence supporting this claim, see Benjamin M. Friedman, *The Moral Consequences of Economic Growth* (New York: Knopf, 2005). The problem is not wealth itself but excessive inequality and sharp differences in social power that inhibit the ability of people to make moral claims on each other. I discuss this in more detail in chapter 8.

16. Sociologist Robert Putnam argues that we are in fact withdrawing from social institutions that provide social capital and enable social trust. See Robert D. Putnam, *Bowling Alone: The Collapse and Revival of American Community* (New York: Simon & Schuster, 2000).

17. According to a report by the Pew Center at the start of 2008, 2,319,258 adults were held in American prisons or jails, or one in every 99.1 men and women. See "Pew Public Safety Performance Project: One in 100 Behind Bars in America 2008," February 28, 2008, http://www.pewcenter onthestates.org/report_detail.aspx?id=35904 (accessed April 20, 2008). For comparisons of the incarceration rates of various countries, see Roy Walmsey, "World Prison Population List," 7th ed., International Centre for Prison Studies, King's College, London, 2007, http://nicic.org/Features/ Library/?CORP=King's%20College%20London.%20International%20

Centre%20for%20Prison%20Studies%20(London,%20England) (accessed January 2, 2009).

CHAPTER 4

1. Hannah Arendt, *Eichmann in Jerusalem: A Report on the Banality of Evil* (Gloucester, MA: Peter Smith, 2004).

2. For Zimbardo's account of this experiment, see Philip Zimbardo, *The Lucifer Effect: How Good People Turn Evil* (New York: Random House, March 2007).

3. See the Pew Gobal Attitudes Project for periodic reports on global attitudes toward the United States, http://pewglobal.org/ (accessed June 28, 2008).

4. Conservatives have advanced the theory of the unitary executive for many years, especially the Federalist Society, an organization of attorneys and legal experts devoted to advancing conservative interpretations of the law. Article II of the US Constitution states that the president "shall take care that the laws be faithfully executed." The theory of the unitary executive asserts that the president thus has authority independently of Congress or the judiciary to interpret the law. President Bush used this alleged authority to issue signing statements, assertions of his own interpretations of bills signed into law that he claimed overrode congressional intent. Among constitutional scholars, the unitary executive is not a widely accepted theory of presidential power.

CHAPTER 5

1. See Harris Poll, "Harris Polls Show Democrats Maintain Their Nine Point Lead over Republicans," January 17, 2008, http://www.harris interactive.com/harris_poll/index.asp?PID=860 (accessed June 28, 2008). Although polls show a resurgence in Democratic Party registration, and some decline in conservative identification, voters identifying as liberal remain only 20 percent of the voting public, a number that has been consistent for many years and seems not to be influenced by the failures of conservatism.

2. For survey data showing support for liberal positions on issues, see Robert Reich, *Reason: Why Liberals Will Win the Battle for America* (New York: Knopf, 2004), appendix A.

3. For an account of the response of white voters in the South to civil rights legislation, see Paul Krugman, *The Conscience of a Liberal* (New York: Norton, 2007), esp. chapter 9.

4. For these data see Lawrence Mishel, "Dismal Scientists," American Prospect Online, May 27, 2004, http://www.prospect.org/cs/articles?article=dismal_scientists (accessed August 18, 2006). Data are extrapolated from Thomas Piketty and Emmanuel Saez, "Income Inequality in the United States, 1913–1998," *Quarterly Journal of Economics* 118 (2003): 1–39.

5. For arguments that Democrats ought to make a more religiously focused appeal, see Amy Sullivan, *The Party Faithful: How and Why Democrats Are Closing the God Gap* (New York: Scribner, 2008) and Jim Wallis, *The Great Awakening: Reviving Faith & Politics in a Post-Religious Right America* (New York: HarperOne, 2008).

CHAPTER 6

1. Drew Westen, *The Political Brain: The Role of Emotion in Deciding the Fate of the Nation* (New York: PublicAffairs, 2007), p. 133.

2. This characterization of equality and its connection to autonomy is not without controversy. Many liberals will argue for a more robust understanding of equality that requires an equal distribution of resources or outcomes. I do not wish to rehearse this debate here—I seek an account of the minimal requirements for a liberal point of view.

3. This way of characterizing liberalism is most straightforwardly true of the Kantian and contractarian traditions. Utilitarians, of course, think that we can give an account of the human good in terms of aggregate welfare. However, the problem of interpersonal comparisons of goods precludes them from providing an objective account of human flourishing. Thus, personal happiness for utilitarians remains a subjective matter. More recently, there have been attempts to provide Aristotelian accounts of liberalism that are less reluctant to answer questions about how one should live. My view of liberalism broadly fits into this latter category, which will be discussed in the next chapter.

4. On this issue, classical liberals (libertarians) dissent. Thus, modern liberalism is to be distinguished from classical liberalism. The term "neoliberalism" is also often used, especially in Europe, to describe liberals who prefer little government intervention in the economy. My use of the term "modern liberalism" is intended to exclude them as well.

5. See Pew Forum on Religion and Public Life for data on religion and politics, http://pewforum.org/religion-politics/ (accessed June 28, 2008).

6. This charge was made popular by Allen Bloom, *The Closing of the American Mind* (New York: Simon & Schuster, 1988). It is repeated by conservative writers such as William J. Bennett, *Why We Fight: Moral Clarity and the War on Terrorism* (New York: Doubleday, 2002), and Gertrude Himmelfarb, *One Nation, Two Cultures: A Searching Examination of American Society in the Aftermath of Our Cultural Revolution* (New York: Vintage Books, 1999).

7. The appeal to impartial reason that gives authority to procedural norms is characteristic of much of liberal political philosophy in the twentieth century, especially John Rawls's *A Theory of Justice*, Jurgen Habermas in his many works on communicative action, Bruce Ackerman's *The Liberal State*, and varieties of utilitarianism such as Richard Brandt's *A Theory of the Good and the Right*. There are important differences among these works that I am eliding here but they share a commitment to impartiality as a norm that must govern the justification of political institutions. There is a good deal of controversy about the degree to which the norm of impartiality must extend to political and institutional decision making. Nevertheless, among these works, impartiality is an ideal, a form of reasoning that has special authority that has deeply informed liberal approaches to governance.

8. See Philip K. Howard, *Death of Common Sense* (New York: Warner Books, 1996) and *The Collapse of the Common Good: How America's Lawsuit Culture Undermines Our Freedom* (New York: Ballantine Books, 2002).

9. This criticism of liberalism relies heavily on communitarian critiques such as those of Michael Sandel, *Liberalism and the Limits of Justice* (Cambridge: Cambridge University Press, 1982). See also Michael Sandel, *Public Philosophy: Essays on Morality in Politics* (Cambridge, MA: Harvard University Press, 2005).

10. For a similar criticism of modern liberalism, see William Galston, *Liberal Purposes: Goods, Virtues, and Diversity in the Liberal State* (New York: Cambridge University Press, 1991).

11. See Austin Dacey, *The Secular Conscience: Why Belief Belongs in Public Life* (Amherst, NY: Prometheus Books, 2008) for an account of how attempts to view moral conscience as a private matter backfire on the liberal commitment to freedom of conscience. I agree with Dacey's complaint regarding attempts to privatize conscience, but I think he does not give sufficient attention to the norm of impartiality as the source of what he calls the privacy fallacy.

12. Greenberg Quinlan Rosner Research, "Democracy Corps National Survey," January 22–25, 2006, http://www.greenbergresearch.com/articles/1662/1834_Democracy_Corps_January_22-25_2006_Survey.pdf (accessed June 28, 2007).

CHAPTER 7

1. As I explained in the previous chapter, although the traditions of liberalism take happiness to be subjective, they do not think morality is subjective. Both the Kantian and Millian traditions attempt to give an account of right action rather than human flourishing, and thus seek impartial procedural norms that can regulate society without passing judgment on individual notions of happiness. Mill, to his credit, struggles (without success in my judgment) against the implications of this maneuver.

2. Some liberal theorists in recent years have tried to overcome these limitations by introducing elements of human flourishing into their account of the aim of political deliberation and action. Their work has greatly advanced the cause of reforming liberalism. See especially Martha Nussbaum and Amartya Sen, *The Quality of Life* (Oxford: Clarendon Press, 1993); Martha Nussbaum, *Frontiers of Justice: Disability, Nationality, Species Membership* (Cambridge, MA: Belknap Press, 2006); Michael Walzer, *Politics and Passion: Toward a More Egalitarian Liberalism* (New Haven, CT: Yale University Press, 2006); and William Galston, *Liberal Pluralism: The Implications of Value Pluralism for Political Theory and Practice* (Cambridge: Cambridge University Press, 2002).

3. For a more comprehensive introduction to happiness as voluptuous care, see Dwight Furrow, *Ethics: Key Concepts in Philosophy* (London: Continuum Press, 2005).

4. The idea that care is a fundamental moral motive has been one of the most important philosophical developments to come out of feminist philosophy, although the particular way I develop it here as a species of a revised Aristotelian view is controversial. The seminal work in the ethics of care is Nel Noddings, *Caring: A Feminine Approach to Ethics and Moral Education*, 2nd ed. (Berkeley: University of California Press, 2003). For more recent treatments, see Virginia Held, *The Ethics of Care: Personal, Political, and Global* (New York: Oxford University Press, 2006) and Michael Slote, *The Ethics of Care and Empathy* (London: Routledge, 2007).

5. For evidence that autonomy is the most important value for Americans, see Alan Wolfe, *Moral Freedom: The Search for Virtue in a World of Choice* (New York: Norton, 2001).

6. David Marmot, *The Status Syndrome: How Social Standing Affects Health and Longevity* (New York: Times Books, 2004).

7. The work of Sen and Nussbaum has been especially useful in making this connection between capabilities and autonomy. For references, see note 2.

8. William Gilpin, *Mission of the North American People, Geographical, Social, and Political* (Philadelphia, 1874).

9. Frederick Jackson Turner, *The Frontier in American History* (New York: Dover, 1996).

10. From John Mack Faragher, *Rereading Frederick Jackson Turner* (New Haven, CT: Yale University Press, 1998).

11. See Gary Wills, *John Wayne's America: The Politics of Celebrity* (New York: Simon & Schuster, 1997).

12. Max Westbrook, "Flag and Family in John Wayne's Westerns: The Audience as Co-Conspirator," *Western American Literature* 29, no. 1 (1994): 26.

13. The idea that autonomy must be understood relationally is advanced by a variety of feminist philosophers. See Catriona Mackenzie and Natalie Stoljar, eds., *Relational Autonomy: Feminist Perspectives on Autonomy, Agency, and the Social Self* (New York: Oxford University Press, 2000).

14. For a discussion of the cognitive roots of care as a central component of a liberal morality, see George Lakoff, *Moral Politics: How Liberals and Conservatives Think*, 2nd ed. (Chicago: University of Chicago Press, 2002), pp. 108–40.

15. Gilles Deleuze and Felix Guattari use "rhizome," the scientific term for rootstock, as a metaphor to describe nonhierarchical networks. See Deleuze and Guattari, *A Thousand Plateaus: Capitalism and Schizophrenia* (Minneapolis: University of Minnesota Press, 1987). Any resemblance between their use of the idea and mine is accidental.

CHAPTER 8

1. Much of this chapter is an attempt to trace the implications of Levinas's ethical thought for politics and society. However, it is not intended to be an exposition or analysis of his views. It is more accurate to say that my views are inspired by Levinas's work, closely following his investigation in many respects but departing from it in many ways as well. See Emmanuel Levinas, *Ethics and Totality: An Essay on Exteriority* (Pittsburgh: Duquesne University Press, 1969) and Emmanuel Levinas, *Otherwise Than Being or beyond Essence* (Pittsburgh: Duquesne University Press, 1998).

2. This command issued by the face of the Other is remarkably similar in many respects to what Stephen Darwall calls "second-personal address." See Stephen Darwall, *The Second-Person Standpoint: Morality, Respect, and Accountability* (Cambridge, MA: Harvard University Press, 2006). "A second-personal reason is one whose validity depends on the presupposed authority and accountability relations between persons and, therefore, on

the possibility of the reason's being addressed person-to-person" (Darwall, p. 8). Both Levinas and Darwall share the view that moral authority resides in the other person. However, Darwall argues that his view of moral authority is compatible with the tradition of social contract theory, a position that Levinas would dispute. Although, Levinas and Darwall come from quite different philosophical traditions, the similarities between them are remarkable and their differences instructive.

3. For accounts of equality that distribute capabilities rather than outcomes, see Martha Nussbaum and Amartya Sen, *The Quality of Life* (Oxford: Clarendon Press, 1993); and Martha Nussbaum, *Frontiers of Justice: Disability, Nationality, Species Membership* (Cambridge, MA: Belknap Press, 2006). My argument is that the capabilities for moral address are the most fundamental.

CHAPTER 9

1. The precise definition of "care" is a subject of some controversy in the literature on the ethics of care. There are important distinctions to be made between care as a motive, practice, and virtue. For a helpful summary and discussion, see Virginia Held, *The Ethics of Care: Personal, Political, and Global* (New York: Oxford University Press, 2006), chapter 2.

2. For excellent work on the situation of the family in contemporary life, see Stephanie Coontz. *The Way We Never Were: American Families and the Nostalgia Trap* (New York: Basic Books, 1992); *The Way We Really Are: Coming to Terms with America's Changing Families* (New York: Basic Books, 1997); Arlie Russell Hochschild, *The Commercialization of Intimate Life: Notes from Home and Work* (Berkeley and Los Angeles: University of California Press, 2003); *The Second Shift* (New York: Penguin Books, 2003); Donna L. Franklen, *What's Love Got to Do with It? Understanding and Healing the Rift between Black Men and Women* (New York: Simon & Schuster, 2000); *Ensuring Inequality: The Structural Transformation of the African-American Family* (New York: Oxford University Press, 1997); and Joan Williams, *Unbending Gender: Why Family and Work Conflict and What to Do about It* (New York: Oxford University Press, 2001).

3. Business models of education have been with us throughout much of US history. For a history and an assessment of the business model of education, see Larry Cuban, *The Blackboard and the Bottom Line: Why Schools Can't Be Businesses* (Cambridge, MA: Harvard University Press, 2007) and Kathy Emery and Susan Ohanian, *Why Corporate America Is Bashing Our Public Schools* (Portsmouth, NH: Heinemann, 2004).

4. For a summary of some of the literature on the decline of newspapers, see Russell Baker, "Goodbye to Newspapers?" *New York Review of Books*, August 16, 2007.

5. Even when private interests are not directly funding it, the research can be influenced by financial inducements. In medicine, ghostwriters in the employ of the pharmaceutical industry often write articles in scientific journals and then pay doctors for their endorsement. Journals are subject to pressure by advertisers whose products may be the subject of ongoing research reported in the journal. Companies will sometimes fund symposia and then offer science publishers a fee to publish the articles in a supplement, often without proper peer review. For examples of corporate manipulation of science and a comprehensive account of the dangers of corporate funding for scientific research, see Sheldon Krimsky, *Science in the Private Interest: Has the Lure of Profits Corrupted Biomedical Research?* (Lanham, MD: Rowman and Littlefield, 2003); Richard Horton, "The Dawn of McScience," *New York Review of Books*, March 11, 2004; and Daniel S. Greenburg, *Science for Sale: The Perils, Rewards, and Delusions of Campus Capitalism* (Chicago: University of Chicago Press, 2007).

6. Michael Forsythe, "Bush Tops Clinton in Rewarding Allies with Government Posts," *Bloomberg*, September 30, 2005, http://www.bloomberg .com/apps/news?pid=10000103&sid=aJzwLcLRZiek&refer=us (accessed May 20, 2008).

7. The story of the Bush administration's incompetence and corruption, which extends far beyond the Iraq and Hurricane Katrina debacles, has not yet been comprehensively told. The best summary to date is John W. Dean, *Broken Government: How Republican Rule Destroyed the Legislative, Executive, and Judicial Branches* (New York: Viking Adult, 2007).

8. As we know from the statements of former OMB director David Stockman, the real agenda of Ronald Reagan's tax-cutting frenzy in the 1980s was to "starve the beast," leaving government with so few financial resources that public confidence in government would plummet and Democrats would be unable to pursue their policy initiatives—a strategy that has persisted throughout the Bush administration. Stockman's comments regarding this strategy can be found in William Greider, "The Education of David Stockman," *Atlantic Monthly*, December 1981. For a history of the metaphor and strategy of "starve the beast," see Bruce Bartlett, "Starve the Beast: Origins and Development of a Budgetary Metaphor," *Independent Review* 12, no. 1 (Summer 2007).

9. See Jacob Hacker, *The Great Risk Shift: The New Economic Insecurity and the Decline of the American Dream* (New York: Oxford University Press, 2006).

10. See Joseph Stiglitz, *Making Globalization Work* (New York: Norton, 2006).

11. We already implicitly accept the importance of care in the way we conduct our business. Contracts cannot generate themselves. Contractors will not agree on terms unless they trust each other to hold to their agreement. Furthermore, the efficient execution of contracts requires an atmosphere of trust and considerable interpersonal skill on the part of the contractors. There must be informal mechanisms for anticipating and settling disagreements and this requires negotiations that enable people to make mutual demands on each other and cooperate on finding ways of satisfying those demands. Countless "what ifs" arise that no formal agreement can cover that we must nevertheless handle. Without informal means of settling disputes, contracts must be enforced through the courts at tremendous cost in time and resources. Moreover, we live in a sea of implicit agreements never formalized as contracts that must exist between people if institutions are to function well. Questions such as what is or is not available for public discussion, who can tell what to whom, who is going to take the lead in a situation, whose judgment counts, is a promise absolute or subject to extensive exceptions, how we are to understand the meanings of words, and so on, must be answered and implicitly agreed upon if cooperative activity is to succeed. The success of these informal and implicit agreements rests on the anticipation of needs, perceptiveness in assessing situations, and especially sustained attention to the vulnerabilities of others, all of which are capacities required by the virtue of care that must be supported by the trust that care induces.

12. Masski Imai made the term famous. See Masski Imai, *Kaizen: The Key to Japan's Competitive Success* (New York: McGraw Hill/Irwin, 1986).

CHAPTER 10

1. For a discussion of this issue see Ann Crittendon, *The Price of Motherhood: Why the Most Important Job in the World Is Still the Least Valued* (New York: Henry Holt, 2001).

2. For a discussion of the gender bias built into this way of looking at international relations, see Virginia Held, *The Ethics of Care: Personal, Political, and Global* (New York: Oxford University Press, 2006), pp. 154–68, and J. Ann Tickner, *Gendering World Politics* (New York: Columbia University Press, 2001).

3. Two books are especially useful in surveying reasons for the ineffectiveness of foreign aid. See William Easterly, *The White Man's Burden: Why the West's Efforts to Aid the Rest Have Done So Much Ill and So Little Good* (New York: Penguin Books, 2007) and Robert Calderisi, *The Trouble with Africa: Why Foreign Aid Isn't Working* (New York: Palgrave Macmillan, 2006).

4. A variety of other goods form a commons as well: tangible goods on public lands such as oil, minerals, timber, grasslands, and other natural resources; the broadcast airways, public facilities such as parks, courthouses, and public schools; cultural resources that are not owned by individuals such as books and music in the public domain; and academic and scientific research that is supported by government funding. And gift economies in which no money changes hands but valuable work occurs such as blood donation systems, blogging communities, Linux programmers, and Alcoholics Anonymous form a commons, as does the fount of social trust that all of us rely on for even the most basic activity.

5. Garrett Hardin, "The Tragedy of the Commons," *Science* 162 (1968): 1243–48.

6. For a general discussion of these trends regarding the commons, see David Bollier, *Silent Theft: The Private Plunder of Our Common Wealth* (New York: Routledge, 2002).

7. David Axelrod developed the first iterated Prisoner's Dilemma tournament in the 1970s using computer simulations developed by mathematicians, political scientists, psychologists, and computer programmers. See Robert Axelrod, *The Evolution of Cooperation* (New York: Basic Books, 1985) and *The Complexity of Cooperation* (Princeton, NJ: Princeton University Press, 1997). Various computer simulation tournaments continue to develop more sophisticated strategies. For a comprehensive article explaining a wealth of strategies see Steven Kuhn, "Prisoner's Dilemma," in *Stanford Encyclopedia of Philosophy*, ed. Edward N. Zalta (Winter 2007 ed.), http://plato.stanford.edu/archives/win2007/entries/prisoner-dilemma.

8. This figure is from the International Energy Annual 2005 from the Energy Information Administration, http://www.eia.doe.gov/iea/overview.html (accessed September 9, 2007).

9. See Intergovernmental Panel on Climate Change, "Climate Change 2007: Synthesis Report," http://www.ipcc.ch/pdf/assessment-report/ar4/syr/ar4_syr_spm.pdf (accessed May 10, 2008), p. 20.

10. This assumes that the market is not constructed in a way that provides disincentives to care about the creation of value. It is evident that our current market system, which relies fundamentally on financial institutions to enhance the mobility of capital, has such built-in disincentives. Financial institutions that can move money around with few constraints have no reason to be concerned with whether the businesses they control are productive as long as they can show short-term profit. For a comprehensive account of these disincentives see James K. Galbraith, *The Predator State: How Conservatives Abandoned the Free Market and Why Liberals Should Too* (New York: Free Press, 2008).

11. This idea of a corporation as a community with a higher purpose has been deeply informed by Charles Handy, *The Hungry Spirit: Beyond Capitalism: A Quest for Purpose in the Modern World* (New York: Broadway Books, 1999).

12. Alexis de Tocqueville, *Democracy in America*, (New York: Barnes and Noble, 2003), p. 217. First published in 1862 by Ticknor and Fields.

13. Ibid., p. 218.

INDEX